THERE'S NO FREE LUNCH IN REAL ESTATE

BY JON SWIRE

There's No Free Lunch in Real Estate

Interior Book Design and Layout by
www.integrativeink.com

ISBN 978-0-6152-2277-6
Library of Congress Catalog Card Number: NUMBERHERE

CONTENTS

*Thank You, to the people who helped
make this program a reality:*

*Camille, my true partner and equal, for inspiring
me to become the person I am today.*

*Matt, who tirelessly edited and reviewed every facet of
this book and now knows more about real estate
than he ever wanted to. I can't thank you
enough for all of your help. You truly made this possible!*

*Phil, for knowing the answer to every technical question
and graciously answering them all.*

INTRODUCTION

This isn't some Donald Trump, daddy's money kind of story. I'm like you. In fact, I'm just like you. I wake up every morning wishing I didn't have to go work, wondering what it would be like to own a big house, a fast car and be rich. But I'm not rich. In fact, the only difference between me and you is that I've already started on my journey towards financial freedom and independence. A few years ago I took my $30,000 retirement nest egg, which was the only savings I had, and began investing in real estate. And while I'm not a billionaire, and I still have to go to work everyday, I'm much closer to financial freedom than I ever have been. I still have a mortgage and credit card bills, but I've also turned that $30,000 into a small real estate portfolio valued at $5MM, and I've created a passive income stream of spendable income that totals over six figures per year.

You see, a few years ago I realized that if I was ever going to have the wealth I desired and the lifestyle I dreamed of, I would need to start changing the way I invested my money. Stocks and bonds are great, and everyone should have some money invested in them, but the problem is that stocks generate mostly capital gains and little spendable cash, while bonds provide income but little opportunity for appreciation. I knew that if I was ever going to be able to retire at a young age and have enough money to live on, I would need to find an investment that could create a consistent, passive income stream that continued to work for me even when I wasn't. After all, I hope to one day make the golf course my office. And while I'm not there yet, I know that if I stick to my plan, I'll be able to retire by my mid-40's, working when I want to, not because I have to.

It's funny; if you ask most people how the majority of wealth was created in the United States they'll probably answer "the stock market". And while this was true during the late 1990's, most wealth in the United States, and the world, has been created through real estate. In fact, McDonald's, the U.S. Government, and the Catholic

Church are three of the wealthiest and largest organizations in the world, largely due to their real estate holdings. For the average person like you and me, one of the best ways to create significant net worth and the wealth we desire is through property ownership. This usually means purchasing the home you live in and then expanding your portfolio to include income-generating real estate investments, which will provide the passive income stream you need to retire.

Real estate does just this. It allows you to build a continually growing passive income stream that works for you, even when you aren't. You see, my real estate holdings will continue to generate monthly rent as long as I own them. Most likely, that amount will grow each year if for no other reason than rental inflation. So even if I never buy another property, my annual cash flow will slowly grow over time, generating more and more spendable cash for me to live on. That is one of the greatest benefits of real estate over other investments. The annual passive income stream continues to grow without any help from you. And, you can use that money to pay for whatever you want. Your home mortgage. College tuition. Retirement. Additional real estate purchases. Anything at all. The point is that the funds are there for you to use as you'd like.

The best part is you don't have to be at your desk to earn it. So even when you're on vacation or at the golf course, you're still making money. And no matter how good or bad the economy is, people always need a place to live.

MY JOURNEY

Like I said earlier, I'm just like you. I went to school not knowing exactly what I wanted to do with my life, but knowing that I wanted to be successful. I attended Northwestern University in Chicago and graduated with a Bachelors of Science in Engineering. Engineering never really held my interest, so I never put my degree to use. A few years later I enrolled at The Anderson School at UCLA in Los Angeles where I earned an MBA. After graduation I moved around through a few jobs, but still hadn't found my true calling. What I did know was that I wanted to make a lot of money, have financial freedom, and work my own hours. Really, who doesn't?

It was after leaving my third job out of grad school that my journey into real estate began. I started to read more about real estate investments, and how consistently making the right investments over time, could help me achieve financial freedom. That sounded great. The only problem was many of the books I read just weren't that useful; they talked more about theory and less about practical solutions. In fact, many of them focused on $0 down scenarios, which, I would come to find out, are for the most part completely unrealistic. The one thing I have learned is that there is no free lunch in real estate. I can unequivocally promise you that I can NOT help you turn $0 and into a multi-million dollar portfolio. It can't and won't happen. On the other hand, I can promise that if you invest a small amount of money, perhaps enough to buy your first 2-4 unit property with 10% down, and you are diligent and consistent about your investment plan, you can grow a portfolio that will eventually generate a sizable annual passive income stream.

Even though many of the books I read did not provide me with a clear road to riches, I knew that real estate was going to be my path to millions. So early in March 2001, I took the plunge and purchased my first fourplex (4-unit property) in Los Angeles County. My real estate agent at the time, who was a referral from a friend, mainly focused on residential housing and as I came to find out, didn't really understand much about income property. In fact, looking back I think it's safe to say I probably knew more than he did just from the books I had read, and it was by sheer luck and market forces that my first investment turned out to be a positive one.

Once I had purchased my first property, I was hooked. I realized the power of real estate the first month I received my tenants rent checks. I had enough money to pay the mortgage, taxes, bills, and was still left with a little money for myself. At the time, LA County was in a rising housing market (this was mid 2001) and within 12 months I was able to sell my fourplex for a tidy little profit. I took those funds and did my first 1031 Exchange into two more triplexes (more to follow later in the book on the nuances of a 1031 Exchange). And, it was just 12 months later that I did another 1031 Exchange, this time into 10 duplexes in Texas.

In my first three years of owning real estate, I bought and sold over 20 properties. Since then I've owned single-family homes, duplexes, triplexes, fourplexes, and multi-family apartment buildings. I've also invested in ground-up development deals and condo conversions. I've had the opportunity to invest in many deals all over LA County and the United States. Some of them turned out to be fantastic, and others were not so great. But I've learned that, while not every deal turns out as planned, every deal is an opportunity to learn. I'll share the tools and techniques I've developed so you too can successfully analyze a real estate investment and make the best investment decision for you.

BECOMING AN AGENT & A TEACHER

Once I owned my first property and was hooked, I knew that I had found my calling: Real Estate. For the first time ever, I had found an industry that completely captured my attention. I studied and took the real estate licensing test and joined Re/Max Commercial in Los Angeles, working as a real estate advisor and agent. Since taking the plunge, I've had the opportunity to work with hundreds of seasoned investors. I've been involved in many deals, and have personally brokered over $300 million in purchases and sales. These projects range from apartment buildings to land, to single-tenant NNN properties (explained later in the book) and office buildings. I've worked on deals valued from $200,000 to $110 million and more, with clients including first-time buyers, those who manage multi-billion dollar REITs, and everyone in between. In my first five years at Re/Max I was ranked as one of their Top 25 Agents in the United States and the World. And in 2006, out of over 3,500 professionals, I finished the year as the #3 Agent for Re/Max Commercial in the entire United States.

After becoming a successful commercial real estate agent I began teaching at UCLA Extension in Los Angeles and speaking to local Real Estate investment clubs. My class is titled *Real Estate Investment Analysis* and focuses on helping regular people, just like you, learn how to make successful real estate investments and create life changing wealth. After all, it's real estate, not rocket science. And it really doesn't need to be that difficult. I've written this book and created this program as an extension of that class, combining my real world experience with an academic framework that will help you to understand the real estate market and how to make successful investments, with the goal being to build your own multi-million dollar real estate portfolio that generates a six-figure per year passive income stream.

WHAT'S IN IT FOR YOU?

Now that you've made a commitment to change the way you think about investing and your future, the real question is what's in it for you? My goal is to help you harness the power of real estate so that you can build your own multi-million dollar portfolio generating six figures per year in passive income. I can't promise you'll become rich, but I can promise that if you heed my advice and read this book and watch the videos as often as needed, you'll set yourself on the right track to building your own real estate portfolio and becoming financially free. The only real question left is where do you envision your journey taking you and are you ready to make a commitment to achieve your goals?

I've had the opportunity to watch and learn from many of my clients who started purchasing property in the early 1990s, right after the Savings and Loan crash. Back then, you couldn't give property away, and were often able to purchase property for eighty cents on the dollar, with as little as 10-15% down. In hindsight, you'd probably be willing to go back in time and mortgage everything you owned to purchase anything you could. Yet most people were not buyers and banks were having trouble unloading foreclosed inventory. Some of my clients, as well as a host of other investors with the foresight and knowledge of property analysis in the early 1990s, have definitely reaped the benefits. Since then, throughout the United States, property values have skyrocketed, with a huge surge from 1999-2006. In southern California, prices rose 15-20% annually. A house that cost $200,000 in 2000 was worth $375,000 or more in 2006, leaving some investors with an 800% return on their 10% down payment. My point is, opportunities exist in any real estate market, be it up or down, and if you understand this and the fundamentals of real estate, you can identify those opportunities and take advantage of them to create the life-changing wealth you desire.

WHAT'S NEXT?

The principles contained in this program are illustrated through real-life examples involving projects I've been involved in–either as a broker or an investor. Each chapter draws on information covered in the previous one, and the final few chapters are designed to help you tie it all together. Once finished, you'll understand real estate as an investment and have the comfort and confidence needed to begin your investment career. You'll be able to find deals and figure out their potential investment worth. There is certainly quite a bit of information to process, so take a deep breath, and don't become overwhelmed. Read this book in bits and pieces, and realize that some Chapters will seem more relevant at first than others. Just revisit the Chapters as needed when they become pertinent to that phase of your investing career.

The first step after you've finished this book is to begin your search for a deal. At that point you'll start speaking with real estate agents who'll be your source for potential investments. You'll also begin speaking with mortgage brokers so you can prequalify for a loan and be ready once you find the right property. Throughout the process you'll want to remain patient and refer to this book as needed. Lean on your agent and mortgage broker as well as they'll both be invaluable resources if you've chosen good professionals to work with.

I've had clients make a decision to invest and close escrow on the purchase of a property in as little as 45-60 days. Set a goal for yourself on how quickly you're prepared to go through the information in this book and what your time frame is for finding and buying your first or next deal. One of the most important things you can do is to set goals and create a plan of action to follow. The tools you need to be successful are right in front of you, the only question is when and how you'll choose to take advantage of them. Good luck and let's get started!

Many of the Excel worksheets referenced throughout this book are on the CD included with my program. You can use them for your own property analysis, as well as to follow along with my examples. If you only purchased the book and not the entire program, please visit www.TheresNoFreeLunchInRealEstate.com to learn how you can order the 13 Chapter DVD series which accompanies this book.

CHAPTER 1 - GLOSSARY OF TERMS: A QUICK START

Below is a quick reference of terms and definitions. More detail is provided in Chapter 3, but this will help you gain a quick familiarity with some of the acronyms and terms repeated in the book before you start to read. This list is also provided so you can easily turn back to this page when you need a quick reminder of what an acronym represents or a term means.

1031 Exchange - A "tax loophole" that allows you to defer your taxable gains into the future if you meet the requirements stipulated in Internal Revenue Code 1031. Basically, when you sell a property, you use all proceeds to purchase another property(s) and do not pay tax on any of the gains until a later time (discussed at length in Chapter 12).

CAP Rate - The return an investment would yield if you paid all cash. The technical definition is:

$$CAP \ Rate = NOI \ (Net \ Operating \ Income)/Purchase \ Price$$

The best way to think of a CAP rate is as the 'savings rate' of an income-generating property. If you paid all cash for a 6.0% CAP property, you would earn a 6.0% return on your investment. This would be the equivalent of a 6.0% yield on a CD or savings account at a bank. Note, however, that once you purchase a property using debt, the CAP rate no longer equals your cash-on-cash return, and this will be discussed further in Chapter 7.

DCR/DSCR (Debt Coverage Ratio/or Debt Service Coverage Ratio) - A ratio used by lenders to determine the maximum loan amount a property can financially support. The DCR is calculated as follows:

$$DCR = NOI/Debt \ Service$$

Debt Service is your monthly mortgage payment to the lender.

GSI (Gross Scheduled Income) - This is the gross rental revenue an income-generating property is scheduled to earn before any vacancy loss or expenses are accounted for.

IRR (Internal Rate of Return) - The discount rate that makes the Net Present Value equal to zero. For most investors, the IRR is usually confused with the Annualized Rate of Return as the two are very close in value. This is discussed in greater detail in Chapter 9.

Multi-residential Property - Also called multi-family property or apartment building(s), and is usually considered anything over 5 units, with 2-4 units being referred to as a duplex, triplex, or fourplex.

NNN (Pronounced "Triple Net," and means Net, Net, Net) - Refers to an office, retail, or commercial lease where the tenant is responsible for all costs including real estate taxes, maintenance, and insurance, with the only exclusion being Debt Service payments which would be paid by the owner.

NOI (Net Operating Income) - Your GSI less your operating expenses.

Pre-Tax Cash Flow - Cash flow after all expenses and debt service is paid, but before any income taxes are accounted for.

Refi - Short for refinance.

ROI (Return on Investment) - Your cash-on-cash return based on your total Capital invested, usually expressed as a %. For example, if you earn $10,000 on a $100,000 investment, your ROI would be 10%.

SFR (Single-family Residence) - Acronym for a home or house.

Spec (Short for Speculative) - Usually refers to a risky investment such as a "spec house."

Vacancy Rate (Also referred to as Vacancy Loss) - The rent loss due to a vacant unit(s) during the course of a year, and is usually expressed as a %.

CHAPTER 2 — WEALTH BUILDING MODEL: WHY REAL ESTATE?

*T*he Wealth Building Model - Real Estate vs. Stock Mutual Funds vs. Bonds

When I teach my class at UCLA, I begin each quarter with this simple but powerful question: If you had $60,000 to invest, what asset class would provide you with the best return over a 30 year period? The obvious (or soon to be obvious) answer is real estate. The reason is all of the benefits a person gets from owning real estate, including depreciation, appreciation, passive income, and leverage. The graph and worksheet that follows explains this in dollars and cents, and gives you an easy visual demonstration of why this is so.

This example uses a time period of 30 years, since for most investors, it represents an initial investment made in their early 30s that's left untouched until retirement age. The point is to demonstrate the power of *time* and *compounding* when applied to real estate. Compounding is when you allow your annual returns to be reinvested so that your total, interest-earning principal continues to grow each year. Many of you may have funds invested in a retirement plan such as a 401K or IRA, and know that even though you may only be saving $4,000 per year, that money will grow exponentially over time. The hope is that when you're ready to retire, you've saved a million dollars or more. As inflation continues to erode the spending power of the dollar over time, you need to have saved enough money to be able to retire comfortably. After all, a gallon of milk costs more today than it did 20 years ago.

Let's assume the following annual returns for each investment:

Bonds - 6.5%
Stock Mutual Funds - 10%
Real Estate - 5%

Note that each of these returns is well within historical means - even with market cycles and the current state of the real estate market. For example, The S&P Commercial Real Estate Index averaged a 6.0% annual appreciation rate from 1993 - 2008, and the median home price in the United States increased from $20,000 in 1968 to $218,000 in 2007, averaging a 6.5% annual appreciation rate (according to the National Association of Realtors). Both numbers are significantly higher than the 5% annual growth rate we are assuming in our example. In this sense, the figures are both historically accurate, and conservative with regards to real estate, yet still produce some very powerful results.

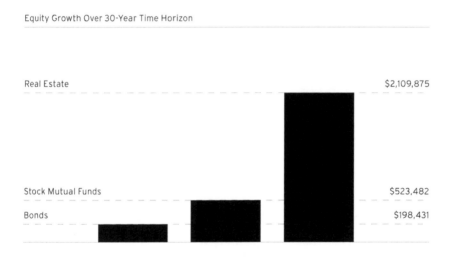

Equity Growth Over 30-Year Time Horizon

Real Estate — $2,109,875

Stock Mutual Funds — $523,482

Bonds — $198,431

As you see, the $60,000 investment grows to just under $200,000 with Bonds, over $500,000 with Stock Mutual funds, and over $2.1MM with Real Estate. Real estate returns over 10 times the amount of bonds and over 4 times the amount of mutual funds, without even considering the spendable annual passive income stream that real estate generates. Money that you can spend every year, on whatever you'd like: a vacation, your kids' college tuition or even another income property. Because this example assumes that you reinvest the annual gains with the Stock Mutual Funds and Bonds in order to produce the given growth, neither generates any annual spendable cash flow for you to use.

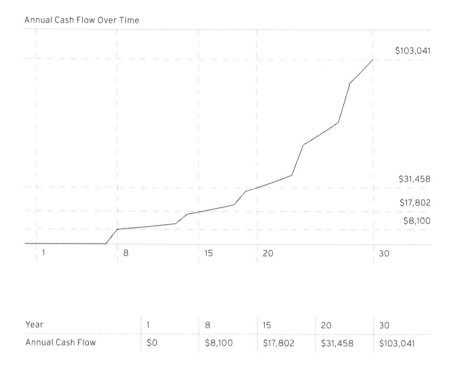

Annual Cash Flow Over Time

Year	1	8	15	20	30
Annual Cash Flow	$0	$8,100	$17,802	$31,458	$103,041

This chart shows you how the annual cash flow from the real estate increases over time, eventually growing to over $103,000 by Year 30, all from a $60,000 initial investment. By Year 30 you'll be earning over a 150% return on your money, in entirely spendable funds. That doesn't even take into account the equity that you're accruing each and every year. This is the power of real estate. It's the only investment that provides you with both income and appreciation. Stock mutual funds and bonds are great, and everyone should have some money invested in them, but the problem is that stock mutual funds generate mostly capital gains and little spendable income, while bonds provide income but little opportunity for appreciation. Real estate provides you with both!

And the best part is come Year 30 you'll own real estate worth over $6.6MM. That's right, **your $60,000 investment will have grown to the point where you now control a $6.6MM asset**, of which $2.1MM is equity. So, how does it work?

5

Step 1: Getting In the Game

The first step is to get in the game and make your first investment. In this case, since we're starting with a small equity investment of $60,000, we're going to purchase a 3-4 unit property. This size property typically won't cash flow positive, but it will allow you to obtain great leverage and stretch your dollars, putting as little as 20% down. So, you're going to take your $60,000 and purchase a $300,000 property. Since you're highly leveraged, the rental income you collect each month will only be enough to pay for all your expenses (taxes, insurance, utilities, etc.) and your mortgage. The property will essentially break even, and your goal is to hold it for appreciation and equity gain. In just a few short years the value will grow to over $400,000, and your equity will grow from $60,000 to over $160,000. Remember, we're assuming a 5% annual appreciation rate (the historical average is 6.5%).

Purchase	Year	Equity	Property Value	Cash Flow
1st Purchase 20% Down	1	$60,000	$300,000	$0
	2	$75,000	$315,000	$0
	3	$90,750	$330,750	$0
	4	$107,288	$347,288	$0
	5	$124,652	$364,652	$0
	6	$142,884	$382,884	$0
	7	$162,029	$402,029	$0

It's important to note that you only want to purchase properties that debt cover even or better. This means that the rental income the property generates is sufficient to pay for all associated expenses (taxes, insurance, maintenance, etc.) plus your mortgage. If a property debt covers even or better you can afford to hold the property for as long as you need to for it to appreciate in value and for your equity to grow. And I think we'd all agree that the value of all real estate will eventually grow over time if for no other reason than inflation.

The main reason many investors lost their properties to foreclosure during 2007-2010 was due to the fact that they were forced to come out of pocket each month to make their mortgage payments. This coupled with the fact that they were underwater on their value - meaning they owed more on their mortgage then the property was worth - forced many investors to decide it was more prudent to walk away from a property through foreclosure than it was to continue to 'feed the alligator' and come out of pocket for the unforeseeable future. Your guiding principle when investing should always be as follows:

Only invest in properties that debt cover even or better.

These charts detail a 30 year schedule showing when you buy and Exchange, how much equity you've accrued, what the value of the property you own is, and how much annual cash flow you're receiving.

2nd Purchase 1031 Exchange 25% Down	8	$150,000	$600,000	**$9,000**
	9	$180,000	$630,000	**$9,630**
	10	$211,500	$661,500	**$10,304**
	11	$244,575	$694,575	**$11,025**
	12	$279,304	$729,304	**$11,797**
	13	$315,769	$765,769	**$12,623**

Step 2: Sell & Do a 1031 Exchange

Once you've built up enough equity, it's time to sell and do a 1031 Exchange. 1031 Exchanges are discussed in great detail in Chapter 12, but the basic concept is that the government allows you to sell a property and defer taxes on the gains until sometime in the future.

This allows you to use the monies you would have paid in taxes to purchase a larger property generating larger cash flows. 1031 Exchanges are one of the most powerful tools available to you as a real estate investor and combined with Cash Out Refinances (discussed in Chapter 9) will allow you to explode your wealth and climb the Property Ladder (discussed in Chapter 13).

In this example you sell your first property in Year 8 and do a 1031 Exchange and purchase a second property. At this point you've accrued about $150,000 in equity that you'll use to purchase a $600,000 multi-family property with 25% down. A multi-family property is a 5+ unit apartment building, and unlike 2-4 unit properties, it will cash flow, mostly due to the fact that you aren't as highly leveraged (25% down vs. 10% down). This property type is discussed further in Chapter 3 &4.

Since this property cash flows positive, you'll have spendable income each year, and during your first year of ownership you'll earn just over $9,000 in pre-tax cash flow. This figure will grow annually, if for no other reason than inflation. Remember, a gallon of milk costs more today than it did 20 years ago, and the cost of everything around you is constantly increasing. You'll again hold this property, and over time it will appreciate and your equity will grow. Within a few years it will be worth over $765,000 and you will have built up over $315,000 in equity. It's then time again to do another 1031 Exchange into a larger property with larger cash flows.

You'll repeat this process every few years and by Year 28 you'll find yourself with $1.5MM in equity, purchasing a property worth almost $6.0MM, generating $90,000 per year in passive income. And by Year 30 the property will be worth $6.6MM, with $2.1MM in equity, generating over $100,000 per year in passive income. All from your initial $60,000 investment. So, are you ready to get started????

Now I realize that some reading this book may not have $60,000 to start with - and that's OK. Your first step then is to put a plan together to save those funds so you can get started. Remember, it's a marathon not a sprint. Sit down and go through your monthly and annual spending budget and figure out how you can start putting aside some money every month and year. This is your future we are talking about and it may require some sacrifice today on your part to ensure your financial future and security. What are you willing to give up in order to start on this path?

3rd Purchase 1031 Exchange 25% Down	14	$300,000	$1,200,000	**$18,000**
	15	$360,000	$1,260,000	**$19,260**
	16	$423,000	$1,323,000	**$20,608**
	17	$489,150	$1,389,150	**$22,051**
	18	$558,608	$1,458,608	**$23,594**
4th Purchase 1031 Exchange 25% Down	19	$540,000	$2,160,000	**$32,400**
	20	$648,000	$2,268,000	**$34,668**
	21	$761,400	$2,381,400	**$37,095**
	22	$880,470	$2,500,470	**$39,691**
	23	$1,005,494	$2,625,494	**$42,470**
5th Purchase 1031 Exchange 25% Down	24	$980,000	$3,920,000	**$58,800**
	25	$1,176,000	$4,116,000	**$62,916**
	26	$1,381,800	$4,321,800	**$67,320**
	27	$1,597,890	$4,537,890	**$72,033**
6th Purchase 1031 Exchange 25% Down	28	$1,500,000	$5,950,000	**$94,500**
	29	$1,797,500	$6,247,500	**$101,115**
	30	$2,109,875	$6,559,875	**$108,193**

Now the example I just detailed doesn't happen overnight. It takes time. But as I like to tell my students, 'slow and steady wins the race'. This is the true benefit of owning investment property. It generates an ever-increasing annual passive income that you can either spend or reinvest; and your underlying principal (your equity investment) appreciates each year— without you doing anything.

The real question is, "How can there be such a huge disparity between these investments?" After all, you're starting with $60,000 in all cases, but the end result is much different. There are a few reasons for the difference in values 30 years from now. They are:

Equity Growth- The equity growth in real estate easily outpaces other investments. Remember, your $60,000 investment in bonds will grow to $198,000, and to $523,000 in mutual funds, but over $2.1MM in real estate. This is due to leverage which will be discussed in further detail.

Continually Increasing Annual Passive Income Stream- No other investment provides you with a growing spendable income stream. Every year, if for no other reason than inflation, the amount of money you collect in rental income is going to grow. This translates into larger checks each month and year to you. That's the beauty of real estate. Your money is working for you even when you aren't.

Further, you can spend that money on whatever you'd like. Your bills, a nice vacation, your kids college tuition, your retirement or even another income property. And, if you decide to save the money instead, you'll be squirreling away a nice little nest egg in addition to the equity you're building in your property.

Annual Appreciation - As a general rule, due to inflation, products/assets increase in value. A gallon of milk bought in 2007, cost much more than a gallon of milk did in 1987. The same is true of real estate. Every passing year, the value of the asset increases. Time is on your side. Real Estate provides you with annual appreciation of the asset, so even though you're spending the annual cash flow and not reinvesting it, the property value and your equity are growing. In this example your equity grows from $60,000 to over $2.1MM as you go from owning a $300,000 property to a $6.6MM property.

Leverage- One of the great advantages that real estate has over other investments is leverage; banks are willing to be your silent partner. It's the ability to use *Other People's Money*. Banks typically invest between $3-$4 for every dollar you invest, and only ask for a flat rate of return in the form of a monthly mortgage. They don't ask for any of your back-end profits, and allow you to put as little as 10% down to purchase a property. For example, in your first purchase you'll be borrowing $4 for every $1 you invest (20% down). And once you do a 1031 Exchange into multi-family properties that cash flow positive, you'll still be borrowing $3 for every $1 you invest (25% down). This allows you to stretch your investment dollars and control a larger asset generating larger cash flows. (As a side note, you can invest in mutual funds using leverage—it's called *buying on margin*. This can be quite risky and only experienced investors should take advantage of this. For most of us, we'll never experience the advantage of leverage when buying mutual funds or bonds.)

Here's an example of how leverage works to your advantage. You invest $60,000 in a stock mutual fund which earns 10% in Year 1, or $6,000. This is your Return on Investment (ROI). Or, you take that $60,000 and purchase a $300,000 property with 20% down. The property appreciates by 5% in Year 1, or $15,000. You just realized a $15,000 gain on a $60,000 investment, or a 25% ROI. Which is better? You see, with real estate you earn the appreciation on the entire asset value, not just your investment. This allows you to build equity faster than any other traditional investment. That is why you're able to accrue over $100,000 in equity in just a few short years in our example. You're earning a 5% annual return on a $300,000+ asset, not your $60,000 investment.

Principal Pay-down - Every month your tenant's pay you rent you use those funds to pay your mortgage, and the principal balance on your loan. Essentially, your tenants are paying your mortgage for you, and on a typical 30-year amortization loan, it takes 30 years for you to pay the balance down to zero. What this means is that in addition to the equity you're accruing from appreciation each year, you're also building up equity through principal pay-down.

Early Withdrawal Penalties/Annual Contribution Limits - Unlike traditional retirement accounts and investments, real estate does not have annual contribution limits or early withdrawal penalties. You can save as much as you'd like, and you can access the funds when you're ready, not when the government tells you. After all, if you plan on retiring early, and before 59 ½, you'll want access to the hard earned money you've saved. Real estate allows this.

Due to the nature of the investment, real estate provides you with a smaller income stream in the early years, but substantial income and wealth due to property value appreciation in the later years, when you're looking to step back from your regular employment and retire. And, unlike traditional retirement accounts, there are no early withdrawal penalties for using the passive income generated on anything you like, at any age. So, if you're ready to step back and play golf all day at age 55, go ahead and do so. After all you've worked hard to save your money and invest wisely, and the passive income stream is available to be spent.

Depreciation/Tax Shield -Every year that you own income property, the government gives you a significant tax incentive in the form of Depreciation. Depreciation is a non-cash expense that will shield part or all of your income every year, increasing your after tax cash-on-cash returns. After all, it's not what you earn, but what you keep.

For example, on an average $345,000 property the government would allow you to shield $10,000 in income every single year, for 27.5 years. What this means is that the first $10,000 in income generated each year would be completely tax free, and you wouldn't owe any taxes at all on that money. If you're in a 35% marginal tax rate, this represents a tax savings of $3,500 per year, and almost $300 per month in additional spendable income. No other investment offers this type of tax shield. Not stocks, not bonds, not money market accounts and definitely not cash.

As we go through this book, we'll explore accounting consequences regarding taxes and depreciation. These are some of the major benefits of real estate and skew the results of this example even further in favor of real estate since both issues are two of the main benefits of real estate over other investment classes.

1031 Exchanges/Cash Out Refis -1031 Exchanges and Cash Out Refis are the tools you'll use to climb the Property Ladder and expand your wealth. Both allow you to take the equity you've built and use it to purchase larger properties generating larger cash flows. And neither has any immediate tax consequence, which means the funds you access are not taxed until sometime in the future, giving you access to them to purchase a larger property with even larger cash flows.

1031 Exchanges are used to sell an existing property you own and replace it with a larger property. These are usually used with properties you're ready to sell and move on from. Cash Out Refis (or Refinances) are used to take cash out of a property by placing a larger loan on an existing property. The additional funds are then used to purchase a second property generating a second cash flow stream.

These are usually used with properties you like and still want to keep as part of your portfolio.

When used in conjunction with one another, these two tools allow you to keep your equity moving and climbing the Property Ladder. After all, your goal is to build a portfolio that will generate a continually growing passive income stream.

So, the next time you're ready to make an investment, think long and hard about where you want your money to go, because real estate provides you with the opportunity to earn extraordinary returns compared to other traditional investments. That being said, you should always maintain a diversified portfolio with your monies invested in different asset classes, with real estate being one of them.

WHY REAL ESTATE?

You're reading this book because you're considering investing in real estate or you've already begun to do so. The question for many of you is, "Where to begin?" The term "real estate" encompasses many things to many people, from single-family houses to apartment buildings, and hotels to amusement parks. Real estate is purchased and held by people for many different reasons including appreciation, tax shields, depreciation, and income generation. Making sense of it all can be confusing and, at times, overwhelming—but it doesn't have to be. This book will help you understand the differences between each type of real estate investment available to you, and the pros and cons of each.

Before we begin that process, you should first identify the reason or motivation behind your desire to invest. I know this seems like a very basic question with an obvious answer—to make money, right??? Well, for many of my clients, that's only part of the answer. Throughout my investment and brokerage career, I've worked with hundreds of clients who use real estate as a means of achieving some larger financial goal. After all, as we discussed earlier, real estate is simply one component of a well balanced, diversified portfolio. And the point of having stocks, bonds, cash, real estate, etc., is to provide for your family and lifestyle. So, the real question is, "What are you trying to achieve in life and how can real estate help you do this?"

Most people evolve throughout their lives and their appetite for risk decreases as they grow older. It's a natural evolution most people go through, even if they won't admit it at first. Think about it, when you're younger, you're willing to risk more to achieve more. After all, when you're in your early 20s and just starting out, you don't (usually) have any children (or other dependents) who count on you; and oftentimes, you don't have many assets. In fact, you probably rent the apartment you live in and lease the car you drive. You may have begun saving in a 401K, but you probably don't have more than $50,000 in net worth to your name, if that. And that's okay. If that is or was your experience, you're like most people in your age bracket; except, you're reading this book and taking proactive steps to improve your lifestyle and future.

As you move through your 20s, you may find that special someone, begin to think about settling down, and start to build a career. Marriage may come, then possibly kids; and before long, you find yourself with a mortgage, two kids, three dogs, and a position in management at the company you work for. All of this forces you to think about your investments and risks differently than you ever did before. If you were investing in your 20s and lost everything, it wouldn't be the end of the world. True, you might have to sleep on a friend's couch, but *everything* at that point might only have been $50,000 or less. You'd still have your job and could rebuild—and, you're only in your 20s with lots of years ahead of you.

Things change once you have a family; and it becomes increasingly important that the investments you make don't bankrupt you or those who depend on you. So, understandably, people go from being in a *Wealth Accumulation* mode to a *Wealth Preservation* mode. Obviously, to get from A to B, you have to first create some wealth worth preserving. That's where this book comes in.

What all of this means is that younger-in-age investors typically take more risks than older investors. And, younger investors typically have different investment goals than older investors. Younger investors like appreciation while older investors like cash flow. For example, your grandmother who's in her 70s is more concerned about income-generating investments than appreciation since she's most likely living on a fixed income comprised of a pension, Social Security, and income from her real estate investments. An investor in his 20s, however, is more concerned about purchasing something that increases in value and creates equity that can be tapped into for the purchase of more real estate and investments.

The first thing I do when I meet with new clients is ask them questions about themselves and their families. I want to understand who they are, where they live, what they do for a living, and what they want to accomplish. Are they married? Single? Divorced? How many kids do they have? Do they have parents/grandparents they need to care for? What other investments do they have? Why are they meeting with me? What do they hope to achieve? What do they hope I can do for them? Before I can even begin to help them, I have to learn about them. I need to know what motivates them and where they see themselves in 5, 10, 20, and 30 years or more.

Once I understand who they are and what their goals are, we can begin to discuss investing, and more specifically, real estate. One of the next questions I ask, and the one you probably thought I would ask first is, "How much money do you have to invest?" For many of you, that's the obvious first question, but it shouldn't be. Instead, you need to spend some time answering the questions I posed above. However you like to take notes, start thinking about your life, where you are today, and where you want to go. What are your goals? How do you see your life changing?

Goal setting is the first step in any investment. The investment you're considering needs to fit into what you're trying to accomplish; and you won't know if it does until you know what your goals are. As crazy as it sounds, and I know it does to some, I began tracking my goals in an Excel file years ago. I probably started when I was 27 and fresh out of my MBA program. I'm a goals-driven and task-oriented individual, so this process seems natural to me.

Every 6 months I sit down and reevaluate where I am and where I'm going. I've created detailed spreadsheets on my current investments and the ones I still want to make. I've put together a plan for how I'm going to achieve these goals and what it will take to get there. I have a good idea of what my investments will be worth when I'm ready to retire, and how much more I need to invest to make sure I retire comfortably. By doing this, I'm able to create my own personal road map to guide me through this process. Every decision I make fits into my plan; and as my life evolves, so does my plan. I realize the investments I make now, in my 30s, are more conservative than the investments I made in my 20s. I'm no different than you are, just maybe a little more organized. Everyone can and should do what I'm doing, if only to secure their future and retirement. To me, real estate investments are a means to an end—simply one part of my overall investment plan to make sure that my loved ones and I are always taken care of.

Investors purchasing real estate typically fall into one of the following categories:

Appreciation Seekers: Those who seek investments that allow their principal investment to grow over time, and

Passive Income/Cash-flow Seekers: Those who seek investments that deliver a consistent cash dividend that increases over time.

The profile of each investor usually varies radically, and generally can be characterized as follows:

Appreciation seekers are typically either younger investors with little net worth or more experienced investors with a high net worth. The younger investors usually seek out situations where they can highly leverage the little funds they do have available, such as 5%- to 10%-down SFRs (single-family residences) or high-leverage 2- to 4-unit income properties. The high-net-worth experienced investor routinely invests some portion of his net worth, but usually no more than 10%-20% in these situations, and seeks what is often termed a *speculative investment* that returns 50% or more annualized.

While the goal of both groups is the same—to quickly increase their equity investment, the profile of each is very different. The experienced investor realizes the speculative and risky nature of these investments and has the cash reserves to weather a down market. The young investor lacks the experience and cash reserves necessary to weather any departure from his original business plan. And if the investment goes south, the young investor oftentimes may find himself in foreclosure.

A perfect example is a client of mine (whom I did not represent in this purchase) who bought a pair of speculative homes in the Palm Springs area of southern California (it's a golf resort/retirement community about 120 miles east of Los Angeles). Both homes were purchased as owner-occupied investments (he put them in the names of his wife and daughter), and both were purchased with 0%-down financing (available at the time in 2005, and much less available as of this writing in late 2007). His plan was to purchase each home for $625,000; spend another $150,000 on rehab for each house; and sell both homes for $1MM or more apiece to net a $100K or more profit on each property.

Unfortunately, the properties were purchased in late 2005, at the crest of the real estate market in the desert; and since then, prices have fallen each month while available inventory on the market for sale has risen. Granted, my client took a property worth $625,000 and upgraded it to an $800,000 property; but had he been able to get to market 12 months earlier, the houses would have been worth $1MM or more. My client tied up most of his available cash in rehab costs, so he was forced to lower his asking price until he found a buyer. This took over 18 months on each property; and he watched his anticipated profit of $150,000 for each home fall to $100,000, then $50,000 and eventually to a loss of $75,000 with each subsequent price reduction. His cash investment of $150,000 in each house, or $300,000 total, turned into $150,000 once both houses were sold, for a net loss of $150,000!

A more experienced investor with proper cash reserves would have been able to hold the properties and rent them out until the market came back. While the properties would not have cash-flowed positive, even if rented, the monthly loss would have been minimal at around $200. My client, however, had most of his liquid net worth tied up in the houses and needed those funds back for living expenses (his daughter was in college and tuition was due). While the market in the desert is weak as I write this, the underlying fundamentals suggest that it will come back in time and his initial vision for the investment will eventually be achieved, just not by him.

The difference in the above example is simple, but significant. The inexperienced investor with little cash over-extends himself. When the market turns downward unexpectedly, these investors are forced to sell the assets they have just to get out from under the monthly payment and free up the cash they do have. My client lost over $150,000 of his $300,000 investment. His Return on Investment (ROI) was horrible. A well Capitalized, experienced investor is able to ride out the market and still make a return at some point, even if it's lower than anticipated. He most likely preserves the initial Capital investment while earning a smaller rate of return 12-18 months later. The inexperienced investor may find himself bankrupt from a situation like this; and if duplicated more than once throughout an investing career, even homeless.

The moral of this story is, Make sure you're prepared for all scenarios. Banks often lend a person more money than he can realistically be responsible for. The qualifying ratios banks use can be very aggressive; and taking advantage of loan programs through false pretenses (purchasing two owner-occupied homes in the names of his daughter and wife), can allow you to take on far more debt than you could ever service at one time. Be aggressive, but smart, and make sure that you plan for the worst-case scenario.

Finally, don't try to make your fortune all at once. Small steps taken carefully can lead to large fortunes. Real estate is not like the stock market. You can't wake up in the morning and watch your stock portfolio value move by 10%-20% or more and then instantly sell and reap the profits. You have to carefully cultivate your investment(s) and make sure you protect the monies you started with and the profits you hope to make.

Finally, real estate is not nearly as liquid as other investments. It requires time and effort to sell; so any decision to liquidate an asset and either pay taxes or do a 1031 Exchange should be carefully planned out.

Rule #1 of Investing: Always get your initial investment back! It's called *Preservation of Capital.*

This rule may seem simple or obvious, and for some of you even ridiculous, but it's true. Most people look at an investment and the only question they ask is, "How much will my return be: 20% or 100%?" They never consider the fact they may not make a return. They've never seen or heard of an investment not making money and can't imagine a scenario that wouldn't.

The truth, however, is far different. Many people have made investments that didn't make money, and getting back their investment was not guaranteed. Preservation of Capital should always be your first priority. You need to get your initial investment back before you can make any money. So, when you look at any deal and analyze it, the first thing you need to do is consider whether it even has the potential to return your investment. Then, do a *Sensitivity Analysis* (discussed in Chapter 9) and consider how wrong things can go, yet still allow you to break even. Breaking even is considered the "worst" situation that still allows you to get your investment back.

Real estate can provide returns for you in multiple ways. The first, and most obvious, is by returning a steady cash-on-cash yield that (hopefully) grows over time. The reality is all income-generating property does this. By virtue of the fact that the lender requires you to meet a minimum Debt Coverage Ratio (DCR) at the time of the loan origination, every property you buy will most likely return at least 2%-3% cash-on-cash if not more (*this is only true of commercial properties and not 2- to 4-unit residential properties*).

There are also real estate investments in projects such as land, condo conversions, redevelopments, and ground-up construction that are more Internal Rate of Return (IRR) driven and usually do not provide any cash-on-cash returns, but rather one lump sum at time of sale or refinance. For example, I invested funds in a new condo development in Florida. At the time of the initial investment, I wrote a check for $200,000; and 32 months later, I was given a check back for $320,000, which represented my initial investment plus a $120,000 gain.

Depending on your investment goals, you might be inclined towards one investment type or the other, and in some cases, both. For my portfolio, I have monies invested in income-generating properties that provide me with monthly cash flow. I can use these funds to pay my home mortgage and bills or save them to use towards my next real estate investment. I also have monies invested in longer-term projects that will provide me with lump sum returns in the future. I've limited my investment in these to a small percentage of my total portfolio (10%-15% in my case). These projects are typically mid-term length in nature (12-36 months) and provide higher IRRs, but come with much greater risk. So, I make sure the monies I invest in these projects are funds I can live without if the investment doesn't pan out, for whatever reason.

If you're a younger investor and earn a good income, owning income-producing property may not be your top priority. After all, you'll have to pay ordinary income taxes on that income, so you might be inclined to invest in something that will return a larger sum in the future without the regular taxable gains. Land and development deals do just that. You invest the money today and have it returned sometime down the road. And, depending on the structure of the investment, you may be able to pay long-term Capital gains on the profits rather than their being taxed as ordinary income (you should always consult your tax professional about this).

As people get older, a consistent monthly income becomes more important; so, investors usually begin to shift their portfolio to income-generating property that can provide them with enough money to live on or supplement a pension, 401K, or other type of retirement account. This is why you see many older investors doing 1031 Exchanges into NNN products that are less management-intensive and provide more reliable income streams since they are shifting to a fixed-income lifestyle.

One strategy some of my investors who own income-producing property use is to take the after-tax cash flow the property generates and put that towards paying down the mortgage early. This way, the property is paid off in 10-15 years rather than 25 or more, and the income substantially increases once there is no mortgage due. For example, if you were in your early 40s, you might set a goal of paying off your mortgage by the time you were 55, and at the point you'd be able to retire and live comfortably off the annual passive income.

CHAPTER 3 — REAL ESTATE BASICS: DEFINITIONS AND PRINCIPLES - WHAT DOES IT ALL MEAN?

As in any industry, real estate has its own language and terminology; and investors and brokers often use acronyms and abbreviations when they speak. The more comfortable you are with the terms, the less time you'll spend wondering what they mean (and mean to you), which allows you more time to focus on the merits of investing. Where possible and necessary, I've included an example or two to further explain meanings. In my opinion, *this chapter is one of the most important in the book* as it provides the framework and foundation for everything that follows. In fact, I suggest earmarking this chapter because you'll most likely find yourself referencing it, as needed, as you move through the remainder of the content.

Remember, the goal here is to help you gain proficiency and comfort. The stronger your understanding is of the following terms, the stronger your ability to act and feel competent. Keep in mind that many of these terms build on others, so I've organized this list in a way that breaks each component down into what it means.

If this section seems a little "weighty" as you read through it—since the lingo may be new to you, it will become a section you rely heavily on once you get serious about investing.

LOI (Letter of Intent) - Usually the first step in the *Offer Process*, and precedes a formal *Purchase and Sale Agreement* (PSA). Typically, an LOI is non-binding and spells out the broad strokes of a proposed transaction including price, deposit amount, and length of due diligence and escrow periods. Most multi-family property transactions up to $8-$9MM usually begin with a PSA. Most deals over $10MM are initiated with an LOI. Most retail and office deals, regardless of size, are initiated with an LOI. The prospective purchaser submits an LOI to the Seller or his/her agent for review. The

Seller accepts or counters those terms. Once both parties agree on general terms, they begin negotiating the PSA and all other points. The total time from submission of an LOI to formal acceptance of a PSA by both parties can take as long as 3-4 weeks, with 2-3 weeks being common.

PSA (Purchase and Sale Agreement) - Legally binding document used to detail the purchase terms of real property.

Multi-residential Property - Also called multi-family property or apartment building(s), and is usually considered anything over 5 units, with 2-4 units being referred to as a duplex, triplex, or fourplex.

GSI (Gross Scheduled Income) - The gross rental revenue an income-generating property is scheduled to earn before any vacancy loss or expenses are accounted for. For example, in a 100-unit apartment building where each unit is expected to rent for $500 per month, the GSI would be equal to:

100 units * $500 rent/unit/month * 12 months = $600,000

Based on the above calculation, the maximum income the owner of this asset could expect to collect would be $600,000. Now in the real world, this probably wouldn't happen since over the course of one year, a 100-unit apartment building would experience some rent collection loss due to vacancy.

Vacancy Rate (Also referred to as Vacancy Loss) – This is the *rent collection loss* due to a vacant unit(s) during the course of a year. The Vacancy Rate is the rate of the loss expressed as a percentage of the GSI. For example, if you had a 100-unit apartment building and 5 units were vacant every month, you would experience the following Vacancy Rate:

5 units/100 units = 5% Vacancy Rate

Your Vacancy Loss due to those 5 vacant units could also be expressed in a dollar figure. In this example your Vacancy Loss would be:

5 units * $500 rent/unit/month * 12 months = $30,000

As it turns out, $30,000 is equal to 5% of $600,000 (the GSI on this 100-unit building).

It's important to note that when you own/operate an apartment building, office building, or any multi-tenant property, your vacancy at any point in time will fluctuate from one period to the next be it weekly, monthly, or annually. For example, in the 100-unit apartment building, you may experience 7 vacant units in the month of January, but only 3 in February and 4 in March. To calculate the Vacancy Rate and Loss for the year (the standard time period most commonly used), you would do the following:

Calculate the number of vacant units by month and add them together (you can figure a Vacancy Rate/Loss for an office building or retail center by replacing units with square feet. For example, you might have 250 SF of vacant space one month and 2,150 SF vacant the next).

Month	# Vacant Units
Jan	7
Feb	4
Mar	3
Apr	5
May	6
Jun	3
Jul	4
Aug	6
Sep	5
Oct	7
Nov	5
Dec	5
Total	60
Avg.	**5**

Once you've calculated the total number of vacant units during the year, divide that figure by 12 (number of months in the year) to get an average. This number is your *Average Number of Vacant Units per Month*. To convert this to a percentage, simply divide this into the total number of units available for rent each month:

$$\text{Vacancy Rate} = 5/100 = 5\%$$

Gross Operating Income (GOI) – Your GSI less your Vacancy Loss. In this example, it would be as follows:

100-Unit Apt. Building GSI = $ 600,000
Less Vacancy Loss (5%) = $ 30,000
Gross Operating Income =   **$570,000**

Expenses - These are the costs incurred to *operate* your income-generating investment. For example, an apartment building will have an annual property tax bill, utility bills (water, power, etc.), gardener, management, maintenance, and other costs. These are subtracted from your total rent collections.

NOI (Net Operating Income) - The basic definition of the NOI is as follows:

GSI - Vacancy Rate - Expenses = NOI

NOI does not take into account your debt service (loan payment).

Pre-Tax Cash Flow – Cash flow generated by an income-producing investment after all expenses and debt service are paid, but before any income taxes are accounted for. Also defined as follows:

NOI - Debt Service Payment = Pre-Tax Cash Flow

Cash-on-Cash Return - The cash return you *earn* on the total investment you've made. For example, if you were to buy a 100-unit apartment building for $1MM and put down 20%, or $200,000, your total investment would be $200,000. If that building were to generate a Pre-Tax Cash Flow of $20,000, your Cash-on-Cash Return would be 10%. It's calculated as follows:

Cash-on-Cash Return = Pre-Tax Cash Flow/Down Payment
(Investment)

In this example, I've assumed you did not have any closing costs (these might include loan broker fees, title, escrow, and taxes). If you do, you'd add these to your down payment to arrive at your total investment. So, if you incurred $20,000 in closing costs, your total investment would be $220,000.

GRM (Gross Rent Multiplier) - The basic definition is as follows:

Purchase Price/GSI = GRM

For example, on a 100-unit building that costs $1MM and has a GSI of $100,000, the GRM would be equal to 10.0:

$$\$1,000,000/\$100,000 = \mathbf{10.0}$$

Many investors like to use the GRM as a financial metric on apartment/multi-residential properties. It's a simple, easy calculation that can often be figured in one's head. It's also a metric not open to interpretation since, unlike a CAP rate, it's NOT dependent on the expense load of the property. What this means is that the GRM you calculate versus the GRM someone else calculates can NOT vary. Both parties use definitive values since the Purchase Price and GSI of the property will be the same for everyone. As a rule, the lower the GRM of a property, the higher the CAP rate and the better the Return on Investment (ROI) will be. So, if you are considering two multi-family properties, and one has a GRM of 10.2 and the other a GRM of 11.5, the property with the 10.2 GRM will most likely have a higher ROI and be the stronger investment.

As explained above, the CAP rate of a property is dependent on the total expenses (since the NOI is equal to the GOI less the expenses). Expenses are an item that are open to interpretation and can be calculated differently from one person/operator/investor to the next. While the annual real estate taxes cannot vary from one owner to the next, the total management costs can. For example, Investor A may own his/her own investment company and spend only 4% of the GSI on management, while Investor B may have to contract management out to a third-party company and spends 6% of the GSI on management. This is reflected in each Investor's CAP rate; and Investor A will have a higher (better) CAP rate as a result.

What this means is that you need to be very careful when using CAP rates to compare investments, and make sure you fully understand how they were calculated and by whom. Sellers and brokers traditionally tend to underestimate expenses to artificially inflate CAP rates and make an investment appear stronger than it truly is. Conversely, buyers often overestimate expenses, thereby driving down CAP rates, making an investment seem less healthy than it is. My suggestion is for you to always calculate CAP rates yourself when looking at investments. This way, you're the one figuring out what the expenses will be, and your CAP rates will have the same over/underestimation from one investment to the next.

GIM (Gross Income Multiplier) - Same as the GRM, and can be used interchangeably.

DCR (Debt Coverage Ratio) - A *ratio* used by lenders to determine the *maximum loan amount a property can financially support.* The DCR is calculated as follows:

$$DCR = NOI/Debt\ Service$$

Lenders usually want a minimum DCR of 1.15-1.20 on a purchase loan, meaning that the NOI of the property is at least 115%-120% greater than the debt service payment.

DSCR (Debt Service Coverage Ratio) - Same as a DCR; however, some lenders prefer this term to DCR.

Qualifying Rate - This is the *interest rate* a lender uses to calculate how large of a loan a property's NOI can support. This rate may vary from the rate the bank gives you on your loan. For example, you might purchase a property with a 3-year bank loan fixed at 5.75%. The bank, however, when calculating the loan amount, might use a 5.95% interest rate as its *qualifying rate.* It's important to know which rate the bank uses since it impacts your loan proceeds. Usually, the qualifying rate will be equal to or greater in value than the actual rate you receive. We'll discuss this more in Chapter 7.

CMBS Loan (Commercial Mortgage Backed Securitized Loan) - Typically a Wall Street funded loan that runs for a 10-year term and has a defeasance (void in whole or in part) prepayment penalty. These types of loans are discussed in greater detail in Chapter 7.

Life Company Loan (Also known as an LC loan) - A loan typically originated by a life insurance company, usually for a 10-year term, and carries a yield-maintenance prepayment penalty. These are also discussed in greater detail in Chapter 7.

S&P Rating - A credit rating issued by *Standard & Poors* for companies, and usually relates to NNN/retail properties. Ratings go from AAA (excellent) down to D (junk). Anything BBB or less is usually considered non-credit worthy. Lenders like to see tenants with good credit ratings. Walgreens is considered one of the best single-tenant NNN deals an investor can buy, due largely to the credit rating of the company, which is AA or better.

IRR (Internal Rate of Return) - Technically, this is the *discount rate* that makes the Net Present Value equal to zero. For most investors, the IRR is usually confused with the Annualized Rate of Return, as the two are very close in value. The Annualized Rate of Return is best compared to the 3-, 5-, and 10-year averages you might see reported for a mutual fund. For example, a mutual fund might report that it returned 11.43% annualized over the most recent 5-year period. This figure is very close to the IRR of the mutual fund over that period. This concept will be discussed in greater detail in Chapter 9.

SFR (Single-Family Residence) - Acronym for a home or house.

Mom & Pop - A term often used to describe smaller/inexperienced owners of property. This is a term brokers frequently use to describe owners of 1- to 4-unit properties, as well as owners of three properties or less. Often, these owners are less experienced than larger real estate owners and rely more on instinct and less on hardcore analysis. Many of my Mom & Pop clients are not well versed in Microsoft Excel and email, and do not understand what an IRR is. There's a perception among owners of larger properties and REITs that Mom & Pop owners don't fully understand the value of their assets and can sometimes be taken advantage of. I've found that while this is sometimes the case, a large percentage of the time, Mom & Pop owners over-value their assets due to their lack of comprehensive market knowledge.

CAP Rate - The basic definition of a CAP rate is as follows:

CAP Rate = NOI/Purchase Price

What this means in English is that the CAP rate of any investment is basically your cash-on-cash return if you were to pay all cash for the building. This means that if you put down 100% of the purchase price and do NOT take out a loan, your cash-on-cash return would be equal to the CAP rate. So, a building that's offered at a 10% CAP would essentially provide 10% cash-on-cash return, if you were to pay all cash. If the purchase price of the property was $1MM, a 10% CAP building would generate an NOI of $100,000 annually.

Now in the real world, most investors usually finance some part of any purchase, and don't pay all cash. So if you finance your purchase and take out a loan, the CAP rate will NOT equal your cash-on-cash return. For example, if you were to purchase the property with a loan of $700,000 instead of all cash, your cash-on-cash return would be 19.3% instead of 10.0%, as illustrated below:

	Scenario #1	Scenario #2
Purchase Price	$1,000,000	$1,000,000
NOI	$100,000	$100,000
CAP Rate	10.0%	10.0%
Down Payment (Equity)	$1,000,000	$300,000
Mortgage	$0	$700,000
Mortgage Payment (Debt Service - 6% I/O)	$0	$42,000
Pre-Tax Cash Flow	$100,000	$58,000
Cash-on-Cash Return	10.0%	19.3%

Note that in Scenario #1 you're purchasing the property with all cash, and therefore you do not have a loan on the property. In Scenario #2, you put 30% down and take a 6.0%, Interest-Only mortgage, which means you're only making interest payments on the $700,000 you borrowed, which equals $42,000 a year.

CAP rates are an effective way to compare one property to another. As the saying goes, it's a way for you to compare "apples to apples." Computing the CAP rate of all investments you consider allows you to compare which investment(s) will provide you with the best return. However, it's important to note that CAP rates do not account for the credit risk of the tenant or other risks, and are NOT risk-adjusted. We'll go into what this means later in the book (Chapter 4); but understand that not every investment is created equal. It's the difference between having McDonald's as your tenant versus the local dry cleaners. McDonald's is a Fortune 50 company with a great S&P rating and stellar credit, while your local dry cleaners is most likely owned by a Mom & Pop with no substantial assets to their name or balance sheet.

NNN (Pronounced "Triple Net," and means Net, Net, Net) - This refers to an *office, retail, or commercial lease* where the *tenant* is responsible for *all costs* including real estate taxes, maintenance, and insurance. There are also NN leases (pronounced Double Net), where the tenant is responsible for all costs *except* the maintenance of the roof & structure, which the landlord is responsible for. NNN leases are favored by investors since they protect the investor from rising costs. In NNN leases, the monthly rent paid by the tenant flows straight to the landlord as his/her NOI since there are no expenses borne by the landlord.

REIT (Pronounced "REET"/Real Estate Investment Trust) - A company or corporation that invests in real estate. The REIT's

27

corporate structure reduces or eliminates corporate income taxes. In return for this benefit, REITs are required to annually distribute 90% of their income which, in turn, may be taxable income for investors. REITs provide the same type of investment vehicle for real estate as mutual funds do for stocks, and are easily traded from one investor to the next. The minimum investment (usually called a "share") is typically $1,000 or more.

Listing Agent - Agent or Broker *hired by the Owner* of a property to exclusively represent him in the sale. Usually, there's an *Exclusive Listing Agreement* executed by both parties that stipulates the amount of compensation (commission) the Agents involved are due to receive upon successful sale of the property.

Buyer's Agent - Agent or Broker *representing the Buyer* in a transaction. This agent is typically compensated by the Seller in most transactions with a Listing Price of up to $8 million or less. Even though this agent represents the Buyer and has a fiduciary responsibility to the Buyer, he is still paid by the Seller as part of the Exclusive Listing Agreement the Seller executes at the time the property is listed for sale. In many transactions where the Listing Price is $8 million or more, the Buyer's Agent is compensated for his services by the Buyer they represent. In this situation the total commission paid to a Buyer's Agent is typically equal to one percent (1.0%) of the purchase price, but can vary by locale; so check with your agent in these situations to find out what the normal practice is.

Selling Agent - Same as a Buyer's Agent.

Pro forma - A term used to refer to a *statement of forecasted income and expenses*. Typically, when you purchase a property, it will have a current income and expense schedule in place. Many investors create a pro forma schedule detailing what they believe to be the rental upside and expense efficiency achievable through improved management and operations. Many multi-family listings offer an investor the ability to purchase a building with "rental upside" that is achievable "immediately." This is usually referred to as the *pro forma income* of the property.

Refi (Short for Refinance) - Occurs when an owner seeks a new mortgage to pay off an existing mortgage. This usually happens for one of two reasons: Either to obtain a new mortgage at more advantageous terms such as a lower rate, longer fixed-rate term, or interest-only payments; or to take cash out (equity) to use for another purpose.

Rent Roll - This is a list of all tenants occupying the property you are considering purchasing. It will usually include the following information: Tenant Name, Current Rent, Move-In Date, Security Deposit Amount, Date of Last Rent Increase, Date of Next Rent Increase, and Expiration Date of Lease.

Marketing Package (Also referred to as a *Property Setup*) - Created by the listing broker for distribution to other agents and potential Buyers; this includes information on the property for sale, as well as financial statements, a rent roll, local demographics, and other relevant information. These can range from basic one-page setups to detailed presentations that are hundreds of pages in length. These are a great place to start when analyzing a deal; but remember, as an investor you want to verify everything presented in these packages for accuracy and arrive at your own conclusions. After all, the Marketing Package was prepared by the Listing Agent to "sell" you on the investment.

Spec (Short for Speculative) - Refers to a project that is shorter and more aggressive in nature. For example, one of my clients is a spec home builder. He doesn't build homes for a specific Buyer in mind, but rather builds what he thinks the market wants and then hopes he can sell it at a profit.

Mechanics Lien - A lien recorded against a property by a vendor who hasn't yet been paid. For example, if you had a roofer put a new roof on your house and you still owe him $1,200, he may file a Mechanics Lien on your property which he'll remove upon receipt of payment. Oftentimes, a vendor about to start a large job will record a Mechanics Lien on the property which will be removed upon successful completion and payment. If there are any Mechanics Liens recorded against a property, they must be paid and satisfied before Title can be transferred to another entity, owner, or Buyer. Liens are typically filed with the local County Recorder's Office.

Spread - *Spread* is the difference between the rate a lender charges you and the Index they use, also called the *margin*. Loans are *priced* by adding a Margin to an Index. For example, the Index on your loan might be LIBOR (London Inter Bank Offer Rate) or Prime, and then the bank will add to that some Margin, say 2.5%-2.625%. So, if at the time of loan origination LIBOR was at 4.5% and the margin being charged was 2.5%, your start rate would be 7.0%, as shown below:

$$4.5\% + 2.5\% = 7.0\%$$

When your loan goes to adjust, the margin won't change, but the index may have moved since LIBOR and Prime move regularly. For example, on a 3-year fixed ARM (Adjustable Rate Mortgage), your rate would be fixed for 3 years and then begin adjusting thereafter. So, in the above example if LIBOR moved from 4.5% to 5.0% by the end of Year 3, your rate would adjust up to 7.5%, calculated as follows:

$$5.0\% + 2.5\% = 7.5\%$$

On residential loans the spread is called the margin, while on commercial loans it's referred to as the spread. Additionally, on commercial loans the spread is expressed in bps (basis points) and is pronounced "bips" — 100 bps is equal to 1.0%. A 225 bps spread is equal to 2.25%. Spreads are discussed further in Chapter 7. (Residential Loans are used for SFRs and 1- to 4-unit multi-family properties, while Commercial Loans are used for all other income-generating properties).

Tenants-in-Common - This is a method of taking title to a property when more than one owner/entity is involved, and is sometimes referred to as *Fractionalized Ownership.* The individuals on title need not own an *equal* share. For example, if you had three partners, one could own 50%, another 30%, and the final partner could own 20%; and each individual's name would appear on the title, such as Sally Q. Jones and Jerry T. Smith.

Accredited Investor - Many TIC (Tenants-in-Common) offerings and other real estate and non-real estate investments are limited to Accredited Investors (discussed further in Chapter 4). This means that the investor must meet certain financial criteria. Below is a summary of the Security and Exchange Commission's definition of *Accredited*:

1) Investor is an Individual. Investor must meet one of the following:

   a) Has $1,000,000 net worth or more (can include house).

   b) Had income of $200,000 for each of the past 2 years with a reasonable expectation of reaching it the next year.

2) Investor is an entity such as an LLC, Partnership, or Corporation. Investor (entity) must meet one of the following:

   a) Have assets of at least $5,000,000.

   b) If assets are below $5,000,000, then EACH of the owners of the entity must be accredited as individuals. (Note that it doesn't matter how small an interest each owner has, each must still be accredited. It also doesn't matter how much money the General Partner or Managing Member has.)

Most investments may have a maximum of 35 Accredited Investors.

Now that you've gotten a basic explanation and, at least, some understanding of the terminology, the next step for you is to learn how to do market research.

Doing Market Research: What you need to know to figure out if you actually want to buy a property.

The first thing you want to do when considering a real estate purchase is to research your target market/area and learn as much as possible about it. You want to find out everything you can about the city or town you're looking to invest in. This includes how the local economy is doing, what public works projects are planned, and what future development(s) is in the queue. Below is a short list of questions to answer before you make any buying decision. While this list is meant to be comprehensive, it's not exhaustive; and there are always other questions you can think of. You want to use this list to address the questions to your satisfaction before you make any buying decision. This helps ensure that you make a wise investment.

How is the local economy doing? One of the most important things for you to ascertain is how the local economy is doing. Is there a primary job source; and if this source were to leave, what would happen? For example, Detroit, Michigan is home to the automotive industry. The city's economy is directly tied to the success of General Motors and Ford; and if anything were to happen to these companies, the city's workforce would be devastated. If you've followed the ups and downs of the U.S. automakers, you know that many cities in Michigan were hit hard in the 1980s and 1990s, and still are today. In fact, General Motors reported a loss of $38 Billion in the fourth quarter of 2007, and has plans to layoff over 74,000 employees. When considering an area to invest in, you want to make sure that the local

31

economy is not dependent on one industry. If it is, you could have a problem if/when that industry experiences a financial hiccup.

What are the local demographics? How many people live within a 1-, 3-, and 5-mile radius? What are the median and average household incomes (HHI)? What is the male-to-female population ratio? What is the ethnic composition of the population? Is the local population growing? At what rate? What is the median age? Is the population getting older or younger? What are the U.S. Census projections for the next 5- and 10-year periods?

Answering these questions helps you better understand the local population composition and plans for future growth. This information is also vital to lenders as they usually like to underwrite loans for properties (especially for retail/commercial) that have a 5-mile radius population of at least 50,000. So, if the local population is either decreasing, very poor, or too small in size, it's a good idea to know this before you begin the loan process. Additionally, you should be concerned that the local population might not be strong enough to support your project. You can visit the U.S. Census Bureau at http://www.census.gov/ for more information on the area you're considering or do an Internet search as new sites pop up daily with great real estate-related information

As a side note, in many cases where the local population is too small (under 50,000) or the average HHI is too low (usually under $40,000), many lenders require the borrower to put more money down, in many cases as much as 35%-40%.

What current and future developments are planned? I always suggest a trip to City Hall to better understand the city or town you're thinking of investing in and to learn about developments planned for the future. Nowadays, much of this information can be found just by visiting the city's website (it may be under City Planning Department). These sites usually tell you about projects currently underway, as well as those being proposed and currently before the City Council for review. This gives you an idea of how many new housing projects are being built, as well as new retail and office centers that will provide more job opportunities. A city with a lot of future growth planned can be a great place to invest.

Just be careful that you also consider how much competition is being developed that may take future business away from your project. For example, if you're buying a 40-unit apartment complex in Texas, and find out a developer is currently working on entitlements for a 100-unit project just a quarter-mile down the road from your property, this could be problematic for future rent and vacancy levels. On the flip side, I purchased an apartment building in Glendale, CA, where a large developer was just months away from beginning construction on a 450,000 SF Lifestyle Center that was going to bring lots of new shopping, restaurants, and entertainment options to the area. In addition to increasing the local tax base and amenities, this project was also going to provide over 1,500 jobs to the local area.

Development, in general, is a positive thing. You just need to make sure that the local economy can support the growth. Many cities go through cycles of boom and bust; and since it takes developers years to plan, fund, and entitle projects, there's generally a lag between demand and supply.

What do local rents look like? One of the most important market research tools you must use is the *rent survey*. Rent surveys of a local area help you determine what the current rental market looks like, how much vacancy there is, and what rental concessions, if any, landlords offer. To do a rent survey, you simply look for 5-10 competing locations and learn more about what they charge, how much space they have available, and how they structure their leases. Oftentimes, you can gather this information by driving the local area and looking for *Vacancy* or *For Lease* signs, as well as using online resources such as www.apartments.com and other websites that offer local rental listings.

You can organize this information in a simple chart or table as a reference used throughout your search and Due Diligence period. Your goal is to use this data to forecast reasonable current rent levels, as well as create future projections based on vacancy and economic trends. The key to any income-generating investment is the current and future source of rental income. So, make sure you spend as much time as necessary on this step and verify your assumptions.

Many cities around the United States have high vacancy rates for multi-family, office, and retail space due to overbuilding. Make sure you fully understand the local vacancy rate and future projects that are in the pipeline for development so you can accurately account for the vacancy factor in your income forecasts. This is one area where I've seen many investors make overly optimistic forecasts they later regretted. Companies like CBRE (CB Richard Ellis www.cbre.com) and Hendricks & Partners (www.hpapts.com) publish quarterly and annual guides detailing local vacancy and rental rates by submarket and product type. You can usually sign up for these by visiting their websites. (Submarkets are smaller markets within a larger market. For example, Glendale is a submarket of Los Angeles County).

I often see listings from brokers showing a pro forma Vacancy Expense/Loss of 3%-5% for most product types including multi-family, office, and retail. The reality is that in most areas around the United States, the local vacancy is much higher. Make sure that when you calculate your NOI for a project, you use a realistic vacancy rate that accurately reflects the market. For example, on the Westside of Los Angeles, the historical vacancy rate for office product is 15.5%, even though most listing packages use a pro forma vacancy rate of 5%. This means that if you were to buy an office building and operate it for a 5- to 10-year period or longer, on average, you'd experience a 15.5% vacancy rate, not the 5% rate the broker suggests in his/her package. That extra 10.5% in vacancy loss every year can equal your annual operating profit.

I've included a list of Internet sites in Chapter 15 that can also be quite helpful when doing your market research. In addition to those sites, I suggest you do an Internet search on the area you're considering purchasing in as new sites with great information you can access for free pop up daily.

CHAPTER 4 — DIFFERENT PRODUCT TYPES: WHICH ONE'S RIGHT FOR YOU?

*I*nvestment property is a broad term that encompasses many different product types. In this chapter, I define and discuss each product type and help you determine which one(s) best fit your investment goal(s), be it consistent cash flow or appreciation. You may decide that diversifying your portfolio over multiple property types is the best strategy. As I mentioned earlier, investing in real estate is one part of your overall investment portfolio; and within your real estate investments, there are multiple opportunities for you to diversify among product types and geographic regions. This allows you to invest some monies in income-generating property (such as a single-tenant NNN) and some in speculative properties (such as SFRs) where you don't expect any cash flow today, but do expect significant equity appreciation over time.

The main property types are as follows:

- Single-Family Residences (Houses) - SFRs

- Duplexes, Triplexes, and Fourplexes – 2-4 units

- Multi-Family Properties - Multi-residential buildings with 5+ units - also called Apartment Buildings

- Office Buildings

- REITs

- TICs

- Single-Tenant NNN Properties

- Retail Centers - Multi-tenant retail centers from Strip centers with 2 tenants to Power Centers with 50+ tenants and 500,000+ SF of rentable space

- Industrial Buildings

SINGLE-FAMILY RESIDENCES

Also known as SFRs - Many younger and inexperienced investors begin their real estate career by purchasing an SFR. There are a few reasons for this, the most prominent being the ability to acquire an SFR with as little as $0 down. This allows an investor to get started with little Capital outlay and little perceived risk. Note that I use the word "perceived" as there is always risk, even if you don't understand it or it's not easily or readily measurable. After all, some investors believe that if you don't have any money invested in a deal, you can't lose money. This, as you will come to find out, is not always the case.

From a management standpoint, SFRs can be quite easy. There is usually only one tenant since there's only one living area to rent; and a residential lease between a landlord and tenant is fairly straightforward. You can download a lease on the Internet from your local Apartment Owner's Association or purchase one through a variety of legal document websites. My suggestion is to *always* use legal forms, preferably from your local area or state, so the contents don't conflict with local laws.

The major advantage of purchasing and investing in an SFR is *leverage*. Since lenders allow you to borrow 90% or more of the purchase price, the total Capital outlay can be very small. This usually appeals to younger investors who generally have little real estate experience and even less Capital to invest. The downside to this is that quite often the rent you're able to charge is not enough to cover all of your monthly expenses. In addition to the mortgage you have to pay every month, there's an annual tax bill (sometimes due quarterly or bi-annually), as well as any maintenance that's required on the property. And, you may or may not be able to charge the utilities back to your tenant (usually depends on the local market and the lease agreement you negotiate).

The reason you're unable to debt cover each month and have the rental income pay for your mortgage, taxes, etc., is due to the basic economics of SFRs.

You're often unable to recoup your total monthly expenses from the rental income because your tenant would purchase the house himself if the rent were more than the mortgage. After all, more often than not, SFR investors put 10% down or less. With the median home price in the United States around $250,000, this equates to a down payment of $25,000. And, even if the tenant did not have the 10% down payment, he could probably purchase the house with $0 down (depending upon his credit and current lending guidelines). Even though he'd have a higher mortgage payment than yours if he put down 10%, he'd gain the tax write-off of home ownership that would more than offset the additional monthly payment.

As you can see, owning SFRs, be it one or multiple ones, usually will not cash-flow positive, and will not even cash-flow *even*, in many cases. The only reason, then, to invest in a SFR is often a lack of available Capital. Your hope is that the value appreciates over time and, hopefully, so does your equity position which oftentimes starts out as nothing.

One final point on the monthly rental income from an SFR is that it's solely contingent on the property being rented. Since there's only 1 unit to rent, if the unit is vacant for any reason, you don't have any *income* during that month or period of time with which to pay your expenses. Vacancy can be a financial killer. Many smaller cities in the U.S. run at an average vacancy rate of 8-12%, which means on an SFR, you'd lose about 1 month's worth of rent to vacancy loss every year. Unfortunately, your mortgage and taxes are still due that month.

Purchasing SFRs can seem like a great investment at first, but you need to be careful of the potential pitfalls associated with them. Let's assume you bought a $100,000 house with 10% down, so you'd be investing $10,000. If over the course of the next 5 years that house were to appreciate by 3% annually, it would be worth approximately $120,000. If you sell that house, you'd realize a gain of $20,000.

Gain on Sale = Sale Price - Purchase Price = $120,000 - $100,000 = $20,000
ROI = Gain on Sale / Invested Capital = $20,000/$10,000 = 200%

That would represent a 200% return on your initial investment of $10,000. Note that this does NOT take into account any buying and selling costs, which can be very expensive and equal thousands of dollars or more. In fact, on a sale, you should realistically budget between 6-8% of your sales price for selling costs. These costs include your agent's commission (usually 5-6%), title and escrow fees, city and county transfer taxes where applicable, as well as termite work and any necessary repairs. As you can see, the amount can be quite costly; and on a $120,000 sale, can be anywhere from $7,000-$10,000, which significantly cuts into your profit.

Sale Costs = 6-8% = $120,000 * .06-.08 = $7,200 or $9,600
Gain on Sale = $120,000 - $100,000 ($20,000) - $7,200 or $9,600 = $11,400 or $12,800

After sale costs you might realize a $10,000-$13,000 gain, which is still a 100-130% return on your investment over a 5-year period. This equates to a 17-22% annualized return, which is quite good compared to many other investments. However, this only happens if/when the home *increases in value*. Every month you own that home, you hope to be cash-flow *even*, not negative. If you go negative every month, even just $100, you need to account for this in your sale proceeds and total investment calculations.

And what happens if the value of the property does not appreciate at 3% per year, or at all? What if the property value stays flat or declines? While this probably would never happen over a 30-year period just due to inflation (which has averaged close to 3% for the past 40+ years), the real estate market is cyclical; and over a 5-year period, anything is possible. In fact, the value may fall by 10%-15% or more. When property values fall, rents usually fall as well, meaning you now have less rental income coming in every month with which to pay your mortgage, taxes, and all operating costs. You may go cash-flow negative which forces you to "feed the alligator" and make up the cash-flow shortfall from other sources be it savings, monthly income from your job, or from other investments. And if, or when, you can't continue to make up the cash shortfall every month, you'll be forced to either sell or go into foreclosure.

When you decide to sell the property (or if you have to), it may only be worth $85,000-$90,000, not the $100,000 you paid. You not only lose your equity investment, but also the sales costs you'll incur just to sell the property. SFRs can provide a great ROI if values increase; but they'll usually never be a source of consistent, steady cash flow and can turn out to be a true disaster if rents decrease and you can't continue to feed that gator.

My final point on investing in SFRs is they can be management-intensive. While owning 10 SFRs and a 10-unit apartment building essentially equates to your having ten renters, each are actually quite different in reality. Often, they're dispersed miles apart, perhaps even in different counties or states, and require much more attention from you. You have ten mortgages and utility/water bills to pay, ten lawns to mow and care for, and ten different properties to keep track of rather than one. You'd need to visit each property with some frequency to check on your investment and make sure your tenants are taking care of your property and not trashing it. There are no economies of scale to be gained in owning SFRs. My suggestion is to limit your portfolio to only a few SFRs, if any, and use the equity gains you accrue to do a 1031 Exchange into a multi-residential property such as a duplex or triplex to start, and then onto 5(+)-unit buildings.

A client of mine owned 18 SFRs throughout the San Fernando Valley of Los Angeles County. I showed him that by selling all his properties and using the funds to do a 1031 Exchange, he could purchase one asset that generated more cash flow each month than all 18 SFRs combined and required less maintenance and supervision. He agreed, and we sold them for a total of $7.5MM, of which $2.5MM was equity. We then used those funds to purchase a $9.0MM apartment building. My client went from having 18 properties to visit, to just one, and he was much happier.

DUPLEXES, TRIPLEXES, AND FOURPLEXES (2-4 UNITS)

The next step up from an SFR is a 2- to 4-unit property. These are also referred to as duplexes, triplexes, and fourplexes (based on the number of units) and are financed with residential loans. This means you can often put as little as 10% down and sometimes as little as 0%-5% down. While 2- to 4-unit properties are similar to SFRs, the main difference is you have more than one unit to collect income from, so no one unit accounts for 100% of your Gross Scheduled Income (GSI). This means that if a unit is vacant for a period of time, you at least have income from the remaining units to help cover your monthly expenses. The income may not be enough to cover them all; but unlike an SFR, you *will* have some.

Since 2- to 4-unit properties are mainly the domain of the younger, less experienced investor, they often trade at very low CAP rates and very high GRMs. When you couple this with the high leverage used to purchase them, these properties are *infrequently* able to cash-flow even or positive. This means that if you don't have the Capital for a large down payment, you need to be prepared to feed the alligator every month and cover the cash-flow deficit.

For example, in 2006 in Los Angeles County, the average GRM for a 2- to 4-unit property in a B area or better was over 13.0. Against realistic expenses, this equates to a 4.0% CAP, and there is no way you can possibly cash-flow even if you put 20% down or less. In fact, you'd have to put down at least 35% just to break even. Of course, most investors who have that kind of down payment are probably going to consider a 5(+)-unit property where the GRM might average 10.5-11.0 with a corresponding CAP rate of 5.5% or better (properties with 5+ units will always be financed with a commercial loan, not a residential one).

As we'll discuss later, the lending requirements on a commercial loan are far different than a residential loan, with the most important difference being that a residential lender is not as concerned with your monthly cash-flow as much as your credit score. A commercial lender, in contrast, is most concerned with a property's ability to generate enough monthly income to pay the mortgage and will require you invest a large enough down payment to ensure that can happen.

Part of the reason that the CAP rate is lower and the GRM is higher on these smaller properties is the ability of the investor to get such high-leverage financing. It allows an investor the opportunity to purchase a property with much less money down than a conventional commercial property requires. Additionally, these deals are usually purchased by less experienced investors represented by residential agents who do not specialize in investment property, but rather owner-occupied SFRs. As such, neither party really possesses a full understanding of income property and the metrics that drive it. My advice is be very careful who you work with when purchasing 2- to 4-unit properties. If you read this entire book before making your first purchase, there's a very good chance you'll know far more than your agent.

Two- to four-unit properties are a great place to begin your investing career and are the stepping stones to larger buildings that include 5(+)-unit properties and other commercial investments. For many investors (myself included), these smaller-unit properties serve as the foundation of a real estate portfolio; and if properly utilized, allow you to do a 1031 Exchange into a larger property. The goal is to purchase your first building with your available Capital; and once you've increased your equity position through a combination of a good management and appreciation, put that equity into a larger property through a 1031 Exchange.

As discussed further along in this book, commercial loans are underwritten differently than residential loans and are far more stringent. Commercial loans typically require a minimum of 20% down; and in some interest rate and CAP rate environments, you can be required to put as much as 35%-40% down or more. Residential loans might only require you to put down 10% of the purchase price or less and are, therefore, far more accessible to the younger investor. Making a 2- to 4-unit property a first purchase lets you get into the real estate game with far less Capital than a 5(+)-unit property would require. Once invested, your goal is to nurture that asset through strong management and maintenance. By increasing rents where possible, you grow the property's resale value.

One of my clients purchased her first fourplex in 2002, for just under $375,000, putting $60,000 down. The property was located in Los Angeles; and by late 2003, had appreciated to $495,000 in value. Rents at the time were rapidly increasing, and interest rates were dropping, which caused values to skyrocket. We decided it was time to sell and use the funds to do a 1031 Exchange. After all sale costs, she netted $150,000 in equity, which she used to purchase a 7-unit property valued at $530,000. She sold that property in late 2005 for $695,000, and used those funds to purchase a 10-unit property for $1MM, which she still owns today. She started out with a fourplex, and within 4 years was the proud owner of a 10-unit property.

I suggest to my younger clients that once the equity in their property has grown enough to do a 1031 Exchange, they consider selling the building and looking for the next one. The goal is to sell at a profit large enough to be able to afford a 5(+)-unit building. Typically, my investors will sell their first 2- to 4-unit building and either 1031 into two more 2- to 4-unit buildings or one 5(+)-unit building. This is obviously dependent on the total equity gain they realize in the sale. If the gain is large enough to cover the down payment required on a 5(+)-unit building, my suggestion is to purchase one and move beyond 2- to 4-unit properties.

MULTI-FAMILY PROPERTIES:

The next step up from 2- to 4-unit properties is a 5(+)-unit building commonly referred to as a multi-family property or apartment building. These properties range in size from 5 units to as many as a few hundred units or more. One of the largest housing complexes in the United States is located in New York, and is comprised of thousands of units among several buildings. You typically see larger buildings or complexes consisting of 200+ units in more rural areas, and buildings of 10-60 units in denser urban settings.

Unlike 2- to 4-unit properties, lenders require multi-family properties to debt cover and cash flow from day one. Essentially this means that the lender requires the property's monthly income to be large enough to cover all expenses and mortgage payments. This means these investments will *always* generate a positive cash flow (income) for you—unlike 2- to 4-unit properties where there's a good chance you'll go negative some months, if not every month.

Most investors start their careers with SFRs, 2- to 4-unit properties, and multi-family properties, with some eventually graduating to other product types. It's not to say that multi-family is not a sophisticated product type; it's just the easiest to understand and operate, and usually the least Capital intensive (meaning it requires the smallest down payment). Tenants (or renters) are usually easier to find and replace in an apartment building than in any other product type, and the leases are the simplest. This allows anyone willing to learn just a little bit of information the opportunity to get involved in this investment and be successful.

The beauty of multi-family property is the ease of the lease agreement between tenant and landlord. It's a few-page document that can be obtained from your local Apartment Owners Association, usually easy to understand, and doesn't typically require the aid of an attorney to negotiate or execute. An apartment lease is usually 6-12 months in length, then goes month-to-month upon expiration of the initial term. At this point, the lease commonly has a provision calling for a predetermined rent increase or allowing for the landlord to issue one.

State and local laws generally play a role in how often and how large an increase can be given to an existing tenant; so make sure you check with them to understand the local ordinances. In Los Angeles City, you can issue a tenant a rent increase of up to 10% with a 30-day notice, and 10% or more with a 60-day notice. Remember, regular rent increases that keep pace with current market conditions accomplish two things: First, your monthly cash flow increases; and second, your property value increases since it's based on the NOI.

The basic lease used for an apartment makes operating one far simpler than an Office Building or Retail Center. As you'll see below, the leases involved in Office and Retail properties can be 20 pages or more in length; and, it's not unusual for it to take months to negotiate leases and thousands of dollars in legal fees to do so.

Leases on most residential properties are typically written for terms of 1 year, and in some instances, month-to-month. It's rare to see a lease for longer than 12 months, unless it's a SFR that might offer a 2- to 3-year lease. Since residential leases are usually for 1-year terms, they vary from most other income property leases in that they usually don't have built-in rent escalations. Generally, a 1-year lease goes month-to-month upon expiration. At that point, you can choose to write a new lease with the tenant or continue on a month-to-month basis. Depending on the local economy, you might issue the tenant a rent increase to keep pace with the cost of living.

It's important to note that in some cities across the United States, there are local ordinances governing *rent control.* New York City and Santa Monica, CA, are probably two of the most notorious cities for this; but there are many cities other than these also subject to rent control ordinances.

Rent control essentially limits a landlord's ability to maximize his/her income from operations. Under the ordinance, and they vary by municipality, the landlord is, as a rule, limited by how much he can increase the annual rent. For example, in Santa Monica, the annual rent increase is tied to the *Consumer Price Index* (CPI). Each year, the City publishes the annual maximum allowable rental increase in August. From 1986-2006, the CPI increased an average of only 2.0% per year, while rents increased a staggering 5.2% annually during that same time in southern California. The Santa Monica ordinance stipulates that as long as the same tenant occupies the unit and does not move out (vacate), the landlord can only issue annual rent increases up to the CPI. Once the current tenant vacates, however, the landlord can rent the unit at the prevailing market rate. However, once a new tenant moves in, the rent control ordinance kicks in and, again, limits the maximum allowable annual increases.

It's important to understand local rent control ordinances, if any exist. If they do not, you're generally free to raise rents on a regular basis at whatever rate the market will bear. If they do apply, it's in your best interest to understand them before you make a buying decision. After all, these ordinances will impede your ability to maximize the value of your property, and in many instances, make it more difficult for you to deal with and evict problem tenants. I always suggest my clients contact the City (usually the Department of Housing) and speak with someone who handles rent control-related questions and issues. By speaking with them directly, you can become familiar with the intricacies of the policy and be better prepared for property ownership.

My final note on owning multi-family property deals with management. Many multi-family property owners, who start their investment careers by buying SFRs or 2- to 4-unit properties, typically manage these properties themselves. As they grow their portfolio through 1031 Exchanges and additional acquisitions, some investors turn to professional management companies for assistance. This is usually due to one of two reasons: Either the investor has a full-time job or does not have the capability of properly managing their entire portfolio.

Management companies typically charge between 5%-10% of gross rental collections each month. In return, they manage the property which includes advertising vacancies to screening new applicants and running credit reports, to handling maintenance issues and emergencies. I personally have used management companies for many of my properties and find that it frees me from the daily tasks of owning multi-family properties so I can focus on the bigger picture. This is not to say that I'm not involved, quite the contrary. I leave the daily tasks to my manager and check in with him, usually weekly, to make sure things are going well and provide direction on larger decisions such as unit remodels, rent increases, and vacancies.

The key with a professional manager is to find someone experienced, competent, and most importantly, someone you trust. You're hiring/trusting them to manage some of your most valuable assets, and it's important they manage the property professionally. I suggest you always ask for and check multiple references; and, hire them for a 3- to 6-month probationary period before you sign a longer-term agreement. Finally, make sure you understand how they charge for their services so that no hidden fees arise. Many companies not only charge a monthly fee based on a percentage of gross rental collections, but also charge each time a unit comes vacant and needs to be rented. It can be difficult to find a good manager; so when you do, make sure you treat them like gold. After all, your success is largely dependent upon the job they do.

OFFICE BUILDINGS

Office Buildings are what they seem: Investment properties that consist of a minimum of one office space/tenant up to a hundred or more. A typical office building investment might consist of 3-5 rentable spaces while a large office building in a downtown area such as Houston or Los Angeles, might consist of 20 stories or more and house 100 office suites or more. Office buildings can cost as little as a few hundred thousand dollars to hundreds of millions of dollars. There are whole investment companies and REITs devoted to buying and selling nothing but office property, such as Maguire Properties and Arden Realty.

Unlike multi-family properties where leases usually run for 1 year or less, lease terms on office space typically run between 3-10 years in length, not inclusive of option periods (explained in the next paragraph). Sometimes you find a small executive suite (usually 200 SF or less) with a month-to-month or 1-year lease term; but for the most part, the minimum lease term will be 3 years. Additionally, you occasionally find a 20-year initial term lease signed by a larger firm for a very large space (i.e., AT&T might sign a 20-year lease for a space their headquarters occupies that encompasses 300,000 SF or more).

In addition to the primary lease term, most leases contain *Option periods*. The purpose of an Option period is to allow the tenant to automatically extend the lease once the primary term expires, at terms agreed to at the time the lease was signed. Options can be automatically exercised by the tenant and the Landlord cannot legally prevent this. Option periods are usually for 3-5 years each, and there are typically 1-3 option periods written into a lease. The rent during the Option period is generally calculated using an index such as the CPI (Consumer Price Index). For example, the rent during the primary term might be $10/SF, increasing annually by the CPI during the Option period. As a side note, the CPI averaged just below 2% annually from 1980-2000. It can fluctuate from 1% to as high as 4% or more (as in the 1970s when inflation was rampant, and as high as 10% or more each year). You can do a search on the Internet to learn more about this and see what the historical and projected figures are (see Chapter 15 for some great websites).

Oftentimes, the rent charged will increase annually during the *Primary term* and *Option periods*. The usual rent increase might be the lesser of that year's CPI, or 2%. In some cases when space is tight and local vacancies rates are low (meaning the available supply/inventory of rentable product is low), the annual rent increases a landlord is able to charge can be greater than the CPI, such as 4%-6%. This is *not* typical, however, and you should expect to see annual rent increases in the 2%-3% range, or tied to the annual CPI.

Office leases usually require the tenant to pay some or all of the operating expenses associated with the property. These expenses include real estate taxes, utilities (water, gas, electric, etc.), janitorial, common area maintenance (CAM charges), and repairs. Leases structured as true NNN leases require the tenant to be responsible for their pro rata share of all expenses, meaning the owner of the property has no expenses whatsoever, and only has to collect the rent every month.

Leases structured as *Modified Gross* or *Full Service* leases require the tenant to pay their pro rata share of certain expenses (but not all) such as property taxes and common area maintenance, but not repairs. In these situations, the landlord has responsibility for certain costs he might not have in a NNN situation. The monthly rent on a NNN lease will be lower than on a Modified Gross lease for the same space because the tenant bears all costs in the NNN situation and, therefore, pays more out-of-pocket costs above their monthly rent. At the end of the day, when you add the rent paid by the tenant plus all other out-of-pocket expenses that might be incurred (CAM charges, taxes, etc.), the tenant usually ends up with the same monthly rental cost, with the difference being in how it's split between rent and expenses.

The benefit of owning an office building is that your tenants hold longer leases than in multi-family properties, and you know that your income stream is going to be more consistent. Since the leases are for longer periods, you can forecast your future cash-flows with much more certainty since you know exactly how much rent each tenant will be paying annually during the entire primary lease term. In 2005, one of my clients purchased an office building comprised of 12,000 square feet of rentable space. Based on the lease agreements in place, he knew the building would be fully occupied until late 2008, with 25%, or 3,000 SF, of the space coming up for renewal.

Another reality is it's more difficult for an office tenant to move at the end of a lease than it is for an individual who rents an apartment. While a multi-family tenant can spend a half day looking for a new apartment, usually within one square mile or less of their current place, it's far more challenging for an office tenant to relocate. Some of these challenges are described below.

Availability of competing space - The first obstacle to moving is to find a new space that's the right size—meaning not too large and not too small. It's not always easy to find space that's configured properly and has the required parking and building amenities as well.

Proximity to current space - The next obstacle is making sure your new space is not too far from your existing space for two main reasons: Your employees and your customers. If you're a medical or dental office, you need to be sensitive to this. Maintaining proximity to your customers or clients is of paramount importance. After all, nobody wants to drive another five miles out of their way because their dentist moved his office; so, it's important you locate your new office as close as possible to your current one. This can sometimes limit the number of available choices. If yours is a traditional office that doesn't have any members of the retail public visiting you, moving too far from your customers is not as large an issue. However, you want to make sure you maintain a central location to your employee base. Otherwise, your office move may cause you to lose some of your valued employees who don't want to increase their commute each day by another ten miles or more.

Switching costs - Another challenge or obstacle to moving, and maybe the most expensive, is the actual cost involved in physically moving to a new space. Not only can it be very expensive to pack everything up, but it can be quite time-consuming. If not done correctly, it can cut into productivity and company profits. Additionally, when you move into a new space, you have to be prepared to pay for the cost of switching phone lines, new stationary, updating websites, etc.

The space you move to may require painting, new carpet, etc. This is referred to as *Tenant Improvements*, or TIs, and can be quite costly. Depending on the level of finishes this can run anywhere from $5/SF to $50/SF or more. For a 5,000 SF office space, this cost can be $25,000 on the low end up to $250,000 or more; so tenants need to be prepared for this expense as well. TIs are usually negotiated with the lease and are paid in part by the Landlord and the Tenant; and, can take a few days to many months or more depending on the extent of work being done.

Office space, like multi-family property, can be classified as A, B, and C. Class A office space refers to new, modern space that was recently built and is fully amenitized. This might include a café in the building, as well as ample parking for all workers and guests (usually subterranean and secure), full-time security, and doormen. Class B and C properties refer to ones that might be older and have fewer amenities. In the Los Angeles market, B and C properties are typically comprised of offices built pre-1990 and may have covered/underground parking or open air/street parking.

And, finally, a word on management: Most office buildings are managed by professional firms. They can be local or national in nature, such as Colliers Seeley and CBRE. These firms typically charge a flat percentage of gross monthly rents equal to 3%-4%. They handle maintenance and tenant issues, as well as help with lease ups when you have a vacancy. It's important to note they charge a leasing commission on the rent up of vacant space (a rent up is when you lease vacant space— also referred to as a lease up). This cost is usually in the 5%-6% range of the total lease value. For example, if a 5-year lease is signed for $1,000 per month, the total lease value is $60,000. The leasing commission is typically $3,000-$3,600. Make sure when you select a firm and sign a management agreement that these charges are specifically spelled out in the contract. As with any vendor, I suggest a probationary period of 3-6 months before signing a longer-term contract, and always check at least 2 references.

TENANTS-IN-COMMON (TICS)

Tenants-in-Common deals, or TICs, as they're commonly referred to, are opportunities for investors to purchase properties they normally could not afford on their own. These deals are also called *fractionalized ownership deals* because each individual takes title as a Tenants-in-Common investor and owns a pro rata share of the property based on his/her equity investment. The minimum equity investment on these deals is typically $250,000-$500,000, but may go as low as $50,000 on some smaller purchases. The appeal of TICs is that a *smaller* investor with $250,000-$1MM in equity can purchase an institutional-quality asset worth $20MM or more. This has become a very popular replacement property investment for 1031 exchanges (discussed in greater detail in Chapter 12).

TIC is a relatively new investment class that began growing in popularity in 2002, due to a change in the IRS tax code. TIC companies (or *sponsors* as they're called in the industry) basically purchase a large asset and then allow individual investors to purchase pro rata shares of the property. TICs are comprised of all different property types from multi-family to office to retail. The most popular is retail and office, but there are many multi-family opportunities as well.

For example, a client of mine had $500,000 in a 1031 Exchange and used those funds to purchase a 10% ownership stake in a $15MM office complex in Texas. The property was a 100,000 SF building with over 30 tenants on 15 floors. It was built in 1995, and considered to be an "A" asset, referring to its construction quality and location. My client's $500,000 investment represented 10% of the total funds required to close the deal. The property was purchased at a 6.5% CAP and was projected to return 7.2% cash-on-cash in Year 1. Based on this, my client expected to earn $36,000 in Year 1, calculated as follows:

Year 1 Cash-on-Cash = $500,000 * .072 = $36,000

TIC investors take title to the property directly; and, the relationship among all co-owners is governed by a structured operating *Tenants-in-Common Agreement* that allows all investors to benefit from the terms. Each investor has certain rights, including the right to receive a pro rata share of the income, Capital gain, loss, deductions, and credits from the property. In this sense, it's the same as owning the property yourself as each investor accrues the same benefits he would if he were the sole investor on title.

Additionally, each investor has the right to sell his interest in the property, the right to encumber his interest, and the right to bring an action to partition the property. Similarly, the other co-owners are not able to force an investor to sell or encumber his TIC interest, because each co-owner usually has the right to determine when and how to benefit from his ownership interest in the real property. The Tenants-in-Common have the right to vote on all major decisions regarding the property including sale and refinance options. They choose a third-party Property Manager to manage daily operations and a third-party Asset Manager that supervises the Property Manager and assists the co-owner with important decisions. Typically, the properties purchased by TICs are large, sometimes out of state, and require professional, experienced management.

TIC sponsors make money at the time of purchase and organization of the TIC. They have very high front-loaded fees due to the way agreements are structured. Usually the firm sponsoring the TIC investment takes a fee equal to 2%-3% of the purchase price. On a $20MM deal, that could amount to $400,000-600,000 or more. In addition, there are legal fees to structure the offering, as well as loan costs and other third-party fees. All together, these fees can equal 4%-5% or more of the purchase price. It's been projected that a typical TIC deal needs to be held for at least 2-3 years just to increase in value enough to recoup all the upfront fees paid at the start of the deal. So, if you're not planning on holding your TIC investment for at least that long, this type of deal is probably not right for you.

That said, many investors have flocked to these deals in large numbers for a multitude of reasons. The first is the quality of the asset being purchased. Many of these deals are for $10-$30MM properties usually considered to be "A" properties of institutional quality. What this means is that they are well located, have solid credit tenants, and quality construction. These are the types of buildings every investor dreams of owning one day but realizes he'll probably never have the equity to purchase on his own.

The second reason TICs are so popular is the ability of smaller investors to get in with as little as $250,000. This makes these investments available to many Mom & Pop investors. The final reason these are so popular is the ease of management. Investors in a TIC deal typically look for something they don't need to manage or worry about; basically, an asset that will be managed and operated by a professional management company. There's usually a 3%-4% management fee budgeted into the operating statement to account for this service, and the investors are all happy to pay it. Unlike some investors that have their own in-house management firms, TIC investors seek the help of others.

TICs are highly regulated by the government and are required to make sure that every investor is an Accredited Investor according to the SEC. The average TIC has 3-7 investors per project, with some larger investments having more. It's important to note that when you subscribe to and invest in a TIC, you and each of the other investors sign an *operating agreement*. Usually, the agreement stipulates the goals of the TIC and how management will occur. The agreement also outlines rules for making decisions regarding management and the eventual sale of the property. Most agreements require a minimum of a majority vote to make a decision; and in some cases as many as 75% of the investors need to be aligned on a decision. Each member gets to vote based on the pro rata share of their ownership and not based on the number of members in the TIC.

Most TICs offer investors a 6.0%-7.5% cash-on-cash return in Year 1, with the goal of increasing the NOI each year due to rent increases. It's important to carefully analyze the operating budget provided by the sponsor as many of the loans have some *Interest-Only* component to them, and this will inflate your cash-on-cash return in those years since you are not making payments on the loan principal. The real key is to see how well the property will operate once your loan payment becomes fully amortized, usually in Year 3 or 4. If you're happy with the projected cash-on-cash return and the underlying fundamentals of the deal, then it may be right for you.

Unlike purchasing a property on your own, the TIC sponsor does all of the heavy lifting for you. They are responsible for all Due Diligence including the property inspection, review of all financial information, local demographics, and competitive analyses. The sponsor also applies for the loan and takes care of all legal and insurance requirements. Typically, the sponsor provides each qualified interested investor with a Due Diligence package containing all of the information on the deal. I suggest you review the information yourself and make sure you agree with their assumptions and findings. You're also welcome and encouraged to visit the site and local area. If something doesn't make sense or doesn't agree with you, do your own research and call the sponsor to discuss the issue. The time for questions is before you commit your funds, not after.

TICs haven't been around for that long so it's difficult to say how they'll operate in the future. Many TIC deals that have been originated have 5- to 10-year CMBS loans on them that will start coming due in 2009 and beyond. It'll be interesting to see how the investors deal with refinance or sale decisions that will have to be made. My guess is it may be difficult to reach a consensus among 3-7 investors who are spread throughout the country, all with different investment goals. As such, I can only wonder whether some investors who were initially attracted to TICs might regret their decision once they realize they can't readily control their own fate.

You can find information on available TIC deals by speaking with your real estate agent or doing an Internet search. There are dozens of companies around the United States that sponsor TICs. Some have been in business for a while (not many longer than 2001/2002), while others are relatively new. You always want to look at their track record and make sure you feel comfortable with them.

REAL ESTATE INVESTMENT TRUSTS (REITS)

One investment available to investors of all "sizes" is the REIT, or Real Estate Investment Trust. *REITs are like mutual funds for real estate.* The underlying asset that REITs invest in is real estate, and they have strict federal guidelines they must follow. Many REITs are publicly-traded entities that you can buy shares in; and a minimum investment can be as small as $1,000. REITs are a great way for you to start investing in real estate until you have enough money to purchase your own property outright, especially since they have to distribute a minimum of 90% of their operating income annually, which means they can be a very good source of annual income.

Unlike a direct investment in real estate, you don't get to participate in any losses or the depreciation of the underlying REIT asset. Many have returned in excess of 20% a year from 2003-2007 (which happens to coincide with one of the most spectacular real estate markets of the past 100 years). In 2006, the S&P REIT Composite Index was up 35.4%, compared with a 15.8% return for the S&P 500 Index.

REITs invest in all types of real estate including, but not limited to: Multi-family, shopping centers, self-storage, industrial, and commercial. Westfield is one of the largest REITs in the country/world (based in Australia) and owns and operates many of the regional/lifestyle malls around the United States. The odds are good that there's one in your town and you've been to it.

The great thing about investing in REITs is you have the opportunity to invest in many different types of real estate in many different locales. You can diversify your real estate portfolio with multiple product types in multiple states. For example, if you think multi-family properties are going to do well in the Southeast, you might invest in a REIT that invests in apartment buildings in Georgia. And, if you're bullish on the retail sector in the Midwest, you might invest other funds in a REIT that buys shopping centers in Illinois.

Anyone who's ready to invest in real estate, but doesn't have enough funds to purchase on their own, finds REITs are a great way to get involved.

SINGLE-TENANT NNNs

Single-Tenant NNN deals are office, retail, or commercial properties that are occupied by only one tenant. Examples include Walgreens, CVS, Jiffy Lube, Taco Bell, Goodyear Tire, Jack-in-the-Box, Burger King, Marie Callenders, and Applebee's. Usually, these properties have drug stores, restaurants, automotive stores, or national chains as their tenants. The leases vary in length from 10-75 years, and will typically have a 10- to 20-year primary lease term with a few 3- to 5-year option periods. For example, Taco Bell normally signs a 20-year initial lease with three 5-year options to extend, all at a predetermined rate. The initial lease usually has either annual (1%-3%) or regularly scheduled rent increases (5%-12% every 5 years). Most drug stores, however, are flat leases during their primary term, which means they do not have rental increases and the rent remains constant throughout the lease.

Single-Tenant NNN deals are great for investors looking for a consistent income stream. Since the leases are for such long periods of time, an investor can know with certainty how much cash flow he'll receive for the foreseeable future. Most of my clients who purchase these types of deals are over 50 years of age and have moved into a Wealth Preservation mode.

RETAIL CENTERS

Retail centers can vary from small strip centers with 2-3 tenants to large Power Centers consisting of 300,000 SF or more of rentable space. The tenants will have leases of varying lengths, with anchor tenants usually signing for an initial lease term of 10 years or more.

INDUSTRIAL BUILDINGS

These properties are occupied by manufacturing companies that build or fabricate something. For example, General Motors has a large number of industrial properties in Michigan where it builds its vehicles.

Most industrial buildings are occupied by only one tenant, and that tenant usually has spent millions of dollars on adding specialized equipment used in its business.

Now that you have a greater understanding of the different types of real estate available, you can begin to think about which one(s) might be best for you.

CHAPTER 5 — THE INVESTMENT DECISION PROCESS: THINGS TO CONSIDER WHEN STARTING OR EXPANDING YOUR INVESTMENT PORTFOLIO

As stated in an earlier chapter, real estate is just one of the many investment options available to you among typical ones such as stocks, bonds, cash, and private equity opportunities, as well as IRAs or a 401K plan. It's important you meet with a financial planner or someone knowledgeable about investing to help you balance your portfolio and decide how much of your investment dollars to allocate to each asset class since your decisions are going to be based largely on your investment goals and tolerance for risk.

For example, cash is considered to be a very safe investment because there's no way for you to lose any part of your investment if you were to keep it stashed under your mattress or in a safety deposit box at the bank. However, the value of your cash decreases each year due to inflation; and over time, your spending power erodes to the point where your cash is almost useless. This is why you invest your funds in the first place—to make your money work for you instead of solely the other way around. You want to at least keep pace with inflation and, hopefully, outpace it so the amount of your principal continually grows.

Typically, the riskier an investment is considered, the greater the annual return. The Capital markets generally reward increased risk with increased returns, which is why bond funds have such small yields (in the 3%-5% range as of early 2008) while successful private equity investments can return 5 times your money or more, or nothing at all (if they fail). Real estate fits snugly in the middle with far better returns than cash and bond funds, but smaller returns than some other more aggressive investments. You can reasonably expect that a real estate investment in a NNN, retail, or multi-family property will return a 10%-20% IRR over a 3- to 10-year hold period. As a point of reference, the average return for the S&P 500 over the past 10 years is around 10.8%, with most mutual funds returning somewhere in that range as well. So, real estate usually outpaces the S&P 500 over time, as well as delivers other tax benefits you may not get from competing investments.

Most investors allocate their funds over a number of different asset classes. Usually, they keep some funds liquid in a cash/money market account. These monies are on hand for everyday living expenses, as well as emergencies. I suggest you maintain at least six months of living expenses in reserve in case of an unexpected illness or job loss. Other monies will probably be directed monthly or annually to your retirement account in the form of a SEP IRA, IRA, or 401K. These funds are usually invested in mutual funds or individual stocks or bonds that you can select and change on a regular basis. Unlike money market accounts and mutual funds, investing in real estate requires a minimum threshold of available cash and can be a difficult goal for most to attain.

I live in Los Angeles where the cost of real estate is astronomical. A typical fourplex can easily cost $900,000-$1,500,000 or more, making it very difficult to acquire your first piece of property due to the large down payment required. I counsel young investors to remain patient and consistent with their savings. It may take you years to save enough for your first investment; but if you put together a plan and stick to it, you'll get there. It's never too late to start saving for your first real estate investment. If you're reading this book in your early 20s, hopefully, you'll begin now and give yourself a great jump-start.

Lately, there's been a lot of talk about investors using their 401K and IRA funds to purchase and invest in real estate. My advice on this is to be careful. Remember, part of the reason you have a 401K or IRA is to safeguard your future. You want to maintain a balanced and diversified portfolio; so I think it would be unwise, in most cases, for you to invest all of those funds in real estate. That being said, if you have a well funded retirement account, you might consider taking 10%-15% of those monies and transferring them to another asset class such as real estate. This is a discussion best had with your financial planner, and one you should consider at length before making any decisions.

Before you make any investment, you should always understand the investment time horizon and make sure you're comfortable with it. The investment horizon is the projected amount of time it will take for your investment Capital to be returned, and how long you're able to wait before that happens. For example, most people who invest in long-term stocks or fund a 401K or IRA have a very long investment horizon. After all, federal law requires that you keep those funds invested until at least age 59½; and if you choose/need to make an early withdrawal, you will be penalized. So, if you start funding a 401K or IRA in your early 20s, your investment horizon is 30 years or more. Since a 401K or IRA is designed to fund your retirement, it should make sense that those funds you invest will be tied up and unavailable for use for a very long time.

An alternative investment with a much shorter investment horizon might be a spec house you buy with the intention to flip within 3-6 months, 12 months at the most. This means that the Capital you invest will be tied up for a maximum of 3-12 months and available for use in another investment relatively quickly.

As you can see, the difference between both types of investments is huge. The longer your investment horizon, the longer your Capital is unavailable to be used elsewhere. This means that if you want to make additional investments, you'll need to find the Capital from another source. Some investors are in the business of churning their Capital and turning it over quite frequently, while others "buy and hold" and let their money work for them over long periods of time.

There are benefits to both approaches and situations where each makes sense. For example, it wouldn't be sound thinking to invest all of your available cash in a long-term investment (say 3 years or more) in March 2008, if you had a large tax bill due in late 2008 with no prospect of being able to pay it. You should always do a quick cash-flow check to make sure that when you invest funds, you're not parting with money you need in the immediate future for bills or living expenses, or as a cushion for emergencies. I created a 36-month cash-flow spreadsheet that I use to track all of my income, expenses, taxes due, and investments. This allows me to see 3 years into the future when planning how to use my money, and account for timing on cash inflows (returns) and outflows (investments). It's proven quite useful over the years and I would advise you to consider doing the same for yourself.

As I said, typically in real estate the shorter an investment's horizon is the more aggressive the project and the returns. This is not always the case, but is definitely more the norm than the exception. I've found, and counsel my clients to expect, that if they're going to invest in a project that's 12 months or shorter, they should expect a larger return. This compensates for the fact they're most likely going to have to pay taxes on the gain at ordinary income tax rates since the money was earned in less than 12 months. And for most of us, the ordinary income tax rate is far higher than the Capital gains tax rate you would have to pay for gains earned over a longer period of time.

Also, it's much less likely you'll be able to do a 1031 Exchange with the proceeds since you only held the property for 12 months or less.

I've chosen to allocate my real estate investment funds over various investment horizons. As in any well balanced portfolio, I have some money invested in aggressive yields, and other monies in more conservative yields. My more aggressive investments are usually in development or spec projects lasting from 9-24 months while my more consistent, less risky yields come from projects with horizons of 3 years or more, and usually 5-10 years or more. For example, a large part of my investable wealth is in multi-family property which I'll rely on to generate a considerable passive income stream 8-10 years from now. As such, I've invested those funds in what I consider to be a very conservative platform so I don't put those funds or my future at risk.

On the other side of the spectrum, I have a smaller percentage (10%-15%) of my investable real estate wealth in more aggressive opportunities that offer yields of 20% or more per year. I realize, however, that these investments are riskier in nature and there is the possibility that the returns will be lower, non-existent, or some or all of my Capital may be lost. Knowing this, I limit my investments in these types of opportunities to money I can live without if it doesn't get returned. This is not to say that I accept failure from the start, but rather that I'm prepared from a cash-flow standpoint if the funds are not returned. You NEVER want to invest funds you can't live without in a risky or aggressive opportunity. Money that you know you'll need in the future for living expenses or retirement should be safeguarded to ensure your financial well being.

When I meet with a client for the first time, they've often already made a decision to start investing in real estate. By the time they call me, they've most likely talked to a friend or colleague who's invested in real estate and realized that they should be doing the same. My job is to help clients find the best investment available that meets their financial goals and investment horizon. To accomplish this, I present them with a couple of options that we rank in order of Good, Better, Best. Since they've already decided they're going to buy something, the decision is never Buy or Not Buy, but rather Which Available Investment is Best Going to Meet My Needs?

The key is to rank each investment based on the most important criteria to the client. Some clients are more concerned with regular, steady cash flow, such as elderly clients who no longer work and live on a fixed income. Others have tax consequences to consider, such as investors who earn a sizable income at their day job. And some just want to see great appreciation and don't care at all about a cash-on-cash return. For this method to be successful for you, you need to sit down with your husband, wife, partner, real estate broker, or whomever else you're working on this with and clearly list and define your goals. These goals serve as the foundation of any/every investment you make in real estate and beyond. Before you can buy something, you have to understand what it is you're trying to accomplish; then, you can design a road map or plan.

In my case, my girlfriend and I have spent many hours discussing our future and what we want out of life. We've discussed where we want to live, how we want to live, how long we want to have to work, and what type of life we want to lead once we stop working. We've used this information to create a detailed spreadsheet of our current and projected financial situation over the next 30-35 years.

In this worksheet, we accounted for the following: Our current ages, current income, projected annual income, current living expenses, projected living expenses, current monies in savings, projected annual savings, current investments, projected future investments, and projected retirement ages. Our goal was to create a road map we could use to help guide us ahead. After all, we knew we didn't want to work forever, but we weren't sure when we could stop working or how much it would cost us to live once we did—and, would we have saved enough money to live the lifestyle we wanted once we stopped working. Remember, no one wants to retire poor and not be able to afford rent or mortgage payments, car payments, grand children's gifts, and life in general.

Once we put this worksheet together, we were able to create a couple of "models" using different assumptions and scenarios. We could see the effect our savings rate had. For example, if we assumed that our IRAs earned 10% instead of 8%, we would have over 20% more money available by retirement age. We could also see that by working three years longer than we planned, we could buy one more multi-family property and have an even better, more secure retirement.

The real benefit from this was our ability to "see into the future" and understand how our investment decisions today would affect our lifestyle tomorrow. We realized that we could stop working sooner than later, but only if we were comfortable leading a less luxurious retirement. We also discovered that if we chose to increase our savings rate today and cut back on some of our monthly expenses, we could retire sooner, or work the same length and retire in better circumstances.

Now I know, for some of you this is going to seem completely ridiculous. After all, you've probably never planned a family vacation more than 12 months ahead, and now I'm asking you to think about the next 30-35 years. It's up to you. It's your future. I can only show you what's worked for me and many of my clients. But if your future, your spouse's future, and your family's future are of paramount importance, I suggest you make the time to give this some thought. I implore you to do the same exercise with your family to gauge your current financial health, as well as help plan for your future. This exercise is not that difficult, but it will take some time. And I think it's most valuable if you revisit it annually to see how you're doing relative to the assumptions you made and the goals you set.

Exercise - Spend some time answering the questions below. Some are very easy, while others will require you to think a little.

What are my life goals? Financial goals?

Is my goal passive income, wealth accumulation, wealth preservation, or a combination?

Am I single or married?

How old am I; my spouse?

How many kids do I have? How old are they?

How much do I have invested in a 401K, IRA, real estate, stocks, bonds, etc.?

At what age would I like to retire?

Will I need to take care of my parents when they get older?

Will my house/residence be paid off when I retire?

How much money will I need or want to live on once I retire?

Once you answer these questions, you can then create your own 30-year worksheet and work backwards. Take the information you know today and figure out if you're on track to achieve the goals you've set for yourself. If not, how much more do you need to save and how can you do it?

CHAPTER 6 – TRANSACTION FLOW: WHAT HAPPENS NEXT?

In every real estate transaction, there's a natural flow of events. Most often, you'll work with a broker or agent who brings potential deals to you to review for purchase. You want to be familiar with the flow of a transaction so you know what to expect at each step and are prepared for the next action that needs to be taken. This chapter outlines the process and explains each step in detail. Of course, you'll only complete the entire process when you finally identify a deal worth purchasing. On many of the deals that your broker/agent presents to you, you'll only work through the first few steps. As you'll see, many of these steps end in a GO/NO GO decision, either continuing down the path towards purchase or ending the deal at that point.

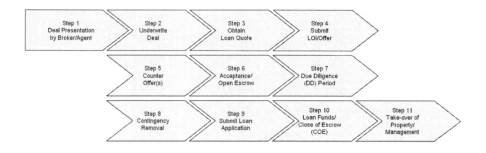

Step 1: Deal Presentation by Broker/Agent - The first step in this process is for your real estate agent to present you with a potential investment opportunity, or deal, to purchase. This usually comes in the form of an email with either a full *Marketing Package* or a *Property Setup*. The full marketing package is usually put together by the Seller's agent (often called the Listing Agent), and contains all the information relevant to the investment in question. A well-done package includes photos, income/expense information, a current rent

roll, a current loan quote, and area demographics. You might also find income/expense projections and rental and sale comparables (Comps). Rental Comps show you what competing properties in the immediate market area are renting for while Sales Comps show you what similar properties in the area recently sold for. Both are vital in helping you underwrite the deal.

Step 2: Underwrite the Deal - Once you've received a marketing package on a potential investment, it's now time for the heavy lifting to begin. It's your job, with the help of your broker, to go through the package and verify all of the information and assumptions provided to ascertain whether this opportunity is something you're interested in pursuing further.

The first step in underwriting a deal is to take all the information provided and transfer it into your own setup. (Chapter 8 goes through a property setup in detail). By doing this, you're able to familiarize yourself with the income and expense streams of the investment and make your own determination of their validity. Once you've created your Property Setup, the next step is to create a *Projected Income & Expense Statement* for your projected hold period (also discussed in Chapter 8). Once this is done, you can compute the project's projected IRR over your hold period (Chapter 9) and determine whether or not the investment meets your minimum return criteria.

In order to verify the income the property can generate, I suggest you do a quick rent survey in the area to verify the current and market rents so you can justify the income on the property. If a rent survey with comparables is included in the Marketing Package, you want to verify that the information is correct and reliable. Your goal in doing the rent survey is to make sure that the current income can be sustained and whether there is potential to increase current rents now or in the future; and if you're able to increase rents, when you can do it and by how much.

You also need to carefully analyze the expense estimates provided to make sure all current and future expenses are accounted for. Listing Agents are notorious for understating and omitting expenses in their setups, thereby inflating the CAP rate and making the investment appear better than it truly is. One of the easiest and most common ways they do this is by omitting a management fee or understating projected maintenance costs.

If the investment looks solid, you move onto the next step which is to obtain a Loan Quote.

Step 3: Loan Quote - Once you've decided an opportunity is worth pursuing, you need to obtain a loan quote to make sure you can obtain financing at acceptable terms since more than likely, you won't be paying all cash for the property. Debt can make or break many transactions, and will be covered in more detail in Chapter 7; but suffice it to say, getting a loan quote early in the underwriting process is imperative. You may find out that the deal is better or worse than you thought based on the available financing in the market. Once you receive a loan quote(s) you plug that amount(s) into the property setup you've created to see how it affects the deal.

For example, I had a client who wanted to purchase a Rite Aid drugstore. Rite Aid is a $17 billion publicly-traded company with a great history and brand. As such, we assumed that a 70% LTV (Loan-to-Value) loan would be available. However, the lender informed us that Rite Aid's S&P credit rating is only a B-, and as such, would require 35% down, not the 30% down we were hoping/assuming would happen. That extra 5% on an $8.4 million purchase was almost $420,000 and was money my client didn't have.

By taking the time to get a loan quote BEFORE we made an offer, we knew we'd need to either raise more Capital or find a lower priced deal. Lenders can be an invaluable source of information and experience. Take advantage of them and listen to what they have to say. Odds are they have seen hundreds, if not thousands of deals and can anticipate future issues and obstacles you may encounter. By planning ahead, you can ensure a smooth transaction and purchase, and most importantly, avoid unwanted surprises. There's nothing worse than going into contract and removing all your contingencies, waiting six weeks for a lender to underwrite and appraise a deal and finally approve the loan, only to find out that the loan amount you requested has *fallen short*. This means you'll be required to come up with a larger down payment than anticipated; and for many younger investors, this can mean disaster since they're already short on cash.

The lesson here is do your homework and BE PREPARED.

Step 4: LOI/Offer - Once you've underwritten the deal and decided that it looks good, the next step is to prepare an LOI or offer, depending on the size of the purchase and the product type. Remember, LOIs are often non-binding documents that outline the terms of a transaction under which a Buyer is willing to move ahead. Unlike Offers, they do NOT bind any party to the terms contained within them even if both parties agree to those terms and sign the LOI. You often find that on multi-family purchases, you go straight to an

Offer, whereas on commercial/retail/office, you often go with an LOI first. However, on deals over $8-$10 million in size, LOIs are most often used first regardless of product type.

I generally prefer submitting Offers over LOIs since Offers can be accepted if all terms are agreed to, and both parties are then bound to the agreement. LOIs can be ambiguous, and often are, and generally only provide the broadest of terms for a transaction. These usually include price, deposit amount, contingency period, and escrow period. Additionally, it's not uncommon for multiple LOIs to be submitted on a property by different Buyers, and for the Seller or his/her agent to be negotiating them all at the same time. In fact, this is a very common occurrence with single-tenant NNN properties. So, where possible, submit an Offer. If you like the deal enough to move to this step, submit something binding.

As a side note, if you're wondering why Offers are binding and LOIs are not, it has to do with the language used in them. LOIs often explicitly state they are not binding to either party, while Offers are usually in the form of binding, legal contracts and explicitly bind each party to certain performance standards. If those standards aren't met, then the other party has the legal opportunity to enforce performance through mediation, arbitration, and litigation, if necessary.

Finally, Buyers typically submit *Proof of Funds* with their offers. This is usually in the form of a recent bank statement that shows the current balance and allows a Seller to verify that liquid funds are available to purchase the property in question. Buyers might also furnish Sellers with a *Schedule of Real Estate Owned* and a *Resume* showing the properties they've bought and sold in the past, as well as the ones they currently own. This lets the Seller know that he is dealing with an experienced, professional Buyer who will perform to the letter of the offer and has the financial means to do so.

Step 5: Counter Offer - Once an LOI or Offer is submitted to a Seller, the Seller typically responds with a Counter LOI or Counter Offer. It's rare that a Seller accepts an offer without countering, but it does occur every now and again. It's more frequent that a Seller accepts the terms of an LOI, and then the Buyer and Seller move together towards drafting an offer based on the terms offered in the LOI. Typically, the offer is in the form of a Seller-drafted Purchase and Sale Agreement (PSA) that the Seller or his attorney has drafted and used before. The PSA incorporates the terms of the LOI and is presented to the Buyer and his counsel for review. Usually, there will be one or two revisions of the PSA as both parties and their attorneys come to agreement on language and terms.

Sellers often counter a Buyer's terms, ranging from price to escrow period, to deposit amounts and due diligence periods. It's not uncommon for a Seller to issue a Counter Offer in response to an Offer, and for a Buyer to issue a Counter Offer (often labeled Counter Offer #2) in response to a Seller's Counter Offer. This can go back and forth as long as necessary until both sides agree; and sometimes, they won't. If you can't agree to the terms the Seller requests or insists upon, you need to move onto the next investment opportunity.

Sometimes, you need to be patient. For example, a Seller may want $1 million for his property, but you're only willing to pay $975,000. Sometimes, time is on your side if the market agrees with you that the building is only worth $975,000. In that case, as long as no one else is willing to offer more than you are, the building will sit on the market unsold. If the Seller is truly motivated to sell, eventually, he'll consider your price and revisit your Offer or last Counter Offer. I've seen many deals die (or "blow up," as we call it in the business), only to be revived weeks or months later when one or both parties came to their senses. The key to a good investment is purchasing the right property at the right price. Patience is a virtue; so practice it when appropriate.

Step 6: Acceptance/Open Escrow - Once the Buyer and Seller agree to the terms of the Offer and Counter Offer(s) and have signed off on all documents, the deal has been Effectively Accepted and escrow can be opened. The date of Acceptance by all parties is considered the *Effective Date of Acceptance*, and is the date from which all time frames in a contract or PSA commence. So, if both parties agree to a 75-day escrow and the Effective Date is August 1, the close of escrow is scheduled to occur no later than September 14th. It's important to note that in all legal matters such as these, dates cannot fall on a weekend, only on a business day. If September 14th is a Saturday, close of escrow is pushed back until the next business day, which in this case would be Monday, September 16th.

Oftentimes, the terms of a PSA require that as part of opening escrow, the Buyer must place an *Initial Deposit* into escrow, typically 1%-3% of the purchase price; although, this does vary locally by custom, property type, and deal size. On a $1MM purchase, the Initial Deposit is usually $10,000-$30,000. Usually, this money is sent to escrow in the form of a Cashiers Check made payable to the escrow holder (it can also be wired from the Buyer's checking account). Once the deposit is in and escrow has a fully executed copy of the PSA, escrow instructions are drafted and distributed to all parties for signature.

In most contracts, this initial deposit is refundable until the Buyer waives his/her contingencies. This means that if the Buyer decides not to purchase the property during the Due Diligence (DD) period, the Deposit is returned, less a small transaction fee paid to escrow for their efforts. In some instances, this deposit may be non-refundable which means that even if the Buyer decides not to purchase the property, the Seller keeps the initial deposit and places the property back on the market for another Buyer to purchase. And sometimes, as is often the case in southern California, a Buyer and Seller may enter contract and open escrow without the Buyer putting down an initial deposit until AFTER all physical inspection and books/records contingencies have been waived by the Buyer. PSAs usually vary by region and local custom, so check with your agent about what the norms are so you know what to expect. It's important for you to understand the timing of the funds required during a transaction.

Step 7: Due Diligence (DD) Period – Once an offer is accepted and escrow is opened, the Buyer enters his/her Due Diligence period. The Due Diligence period is designed to allow a Buyer to review *Title*, as well as the *Books and Records* in a transaction and perform all *Physical Inspections* necessary on the property. The length of the DD period is specified in the PSA and it's very important you adhere to it strictly. Oftentimes, your DD period will be from 7-21 working days, and sometimes more. On smaller deals, 7-21 days is the norm. You must make sure you notify the Seller prior to the expiration of the DD period regarding your intentions to purchase or cancel the transaction. Usually your Initial Deposit will be at risk if you do not notify the Seller and it may become non-refundable. Make sure both you and your agent are clear on the timing, and that you follow the PSA closely or you may risk losing your deposit.

During the DD period, the Seller is responsible for providing the Buyer with all financial information regarding the property, including, but not limited to:

- *Profit & Loss* (P&L) *Statements* for the past 3 years (usually required by the lender, as well).

- *Current Rent Roll* - Showing all current tenants, security deposit amounts, move-in date, date of last rent increase, terms of lease, and any other relevant information.

- *Copy of all tenant leases* - As well as any accompanying rental increase notices (usually relevant to multi-family transactions only).

- *Copy of utility bills* for past 12-24 months (water, electric, gas, trash, etc.) - You want to see all bills which you'll be responsible for paying upon close of escrow.

- *Copy of Laundry Lease*, if one exists (relevant for multi-family property only and only where the laundry equipment is leased, not owned).

- *Copy of Management Agreement* - If the Seller employs a third-party management firm or onsite manager, you want to review a copy of this agreement to understand the total costs involved and which responsibilities are borne by this group, as well as what the cancellation policy is if you decide to switch firms.

- *Copy of Third-Party Vendor Agreements* - Such as gardener, rubbish collection, janitorial, etc.

- *Copy of any transferable warranties* - Such as roof work that may still be under warranty or recent Capital Expenditures that are still under warranty (plumbing, new A/C units, etc.).

- *Title Report* - It's very important that you carefully read through the entire Title report and all underlying documents recorded against a property to make sure that you're purchasing a building with a clean title. For example, you want to know if there are any delinquent taxes due or mechanics liens against the property. You also want to find out if any special covenants were recorded when the property was built, or since that time, that require the owner to conform to certain City codes or regulations. In the city of Los Angles, many apartment buildings constructed in the late 1980s were required to be built with some low/moderate income component to them. Typically, this meant that 15% of the units were required to be rented to low/moderate-income tenants who met certain income requirements. It's important to find this out during the DD period so you can account for it in your income projections. After all, those units usually would rent for far more money at a market rate than they would at a low/moderate income rate.

This covenant could adversely affect your ability to maximize your building's income potential and negatively affect its value.

- *ALTA Survey* -ALTA is short for American Land Title Association. An ALTA Survey is a survey that clearly delineates the lot's boundaries, as well as shows the setbacks, utility lines, easements, and all existing improvements. ALTA Surveys are usually required by lenders to make sure that the existing improvements are legal.

- *Proof of Insurance*

- *EIR (Environmental Impact Report)* - If available; however, more often than not, an EIR does not exist. Depending on the type of loan you apply for, the lender may require an EIR be conducted (typically for CMBS and LC loans). EIRs can range in price from a few thousand dollars or more depending on the size of the project. There's a Phase I, II, and III; and, each is more intrusive and expensive than the next. The EIR is conducted to make sure there are no environmental hazards or issues that exist on the site or beneath the surface. Phase I usually consists of more research and paperwork while Phase II or III require extensive field work and soil samples.

In addition to the above information, a Buyer is allowed to request whatever else he'd like to review, within reason. Your goal during the Due Diligence (DD) period is to verify that the income and expenses reported to you by the Seller are true and actual based on the information you've received. To do this properly, you need to review all of the financial paperwork provided or hire someone to do it for you. You'd typically engage the services of a forensic accountant once the deal becomes complicated or has a lot of moving parts.

As an example, on a 6-unit apartment building, you could review all of the expenses and leases yourself. However, on a 100,000 SF office building with 35 tenants, you'd be wise to hire someone to review all the leases and expenses to make sure there are no hidden problems you'll have to deal with in the future. It's not uncommon in multi-tenant situations (usually office/retail/commercial) for the leases to be very lengthy and complicated, often 25 pages or more in length, and drafted by an attorney. My suggestion is you protect yourself and hire someone who specializes in this area. It will probably cost you a few thousand dollars, but is well worth the cost considering the total size of the investment.

As well as reviewing all of the paperwork, you also want to conduct a physical investigation of the property during the DD period. You can do this yourself or with the aid of a professional. Again, depending on the size of the transaction and your personal experience, you may decide to forgo paying a professional and just walk the property yourself. For example, I have many experienced clients who have owned and operated hundreds of apartment units for years and they feel very comfortable performing their own physical inspections. On the flip side, I have many institutional clients and younger investors who engage the services of professional inspection firms and engineers to make sure they uncover any issues that may exist. The cost to hire an inspector can range from a few hundred dollars for a fourplex to thousands of dollars for a larger property.

You want to make sure you check out the major mechanical systems of the building including the roof, plumbing, electrical, and HVAC units. Again, some of my clients hire individual professionals for each system or ask contractors they have a relationship with to check out the property for them. These inspectors provide detailed reports of their findings, as well as an estimate to make any needed repairs. You hold onto these estimates for future negotiations with the Seller, as well as for when you close escrow and need to make these repairs.

One of the more important tasks for you to do during your DD period is to visit the local City office (usually the Department of Housing) and make sure there are no outstanding citations or violations against the property. You want to confirm that the current owner does not have any deficiencies with the City for work not done due to a recent City Inspection. And, if you find out that there are outstanding items that need repair or attention, make sure you get a complete list so you can present it to the Seller and require him to make the repairs prior to closing.

Once you've reviewed all of the information provided and conducted your inspections, you now need to make sense of everything. Your goal during the DD period is to uncover any potential problems and then determine the time, cost, and effort required to correct them if you still want the property. Some problems you find will be minor and others might be major, or deal breakers, as we call them. Finding out the Seller was off on his total GSI by $125 is not that big a deal, but finding out that the building has major foundation problems that will cost $1MM or more to fix can be. Some things you find will require money to fix, but you may be willing to make the repairs if the Seller will help you in the form of a credit, or reduced price. For example, putting on a new roof or replacing A/C condensers can be costly, but not a deal breaker. Other things you uncover, like a low/moderate income covenant on a property, may be a deal breaker for you, regardless of how large a price reduction a Seller may be willing to entertain. At this point in the deal, you need to sit down and review all of the information you've gathered and decide if you've discovered anything that would prevent you from moving forward with the purchase.

After you've done your due diligence and worked through everything, you can then request a credit from the Seller commensurate with the amount of work required or issues you've discovered, or cancel the deal entirely if it no longer makes sense or the Seller is unwilling to renegotiate. Either way, you need to make sure that you've answered all the questions that are important to you and conducted a thorough investigation of the property.

Step 8: Contingency Removal – (This usually consists of your Physical Contingency, Books & Records Contingency, Title Contingency, and in some cases, your Financing Contingency.) Once you've done your homework during the DD period and your time has expired, it's time for you to make a decision to move forward or not. And if you decide to move forward, you determine if you want/need to request a credit from the Seller for anything you've discovered during the DD period. If you've decided you don't want to purchase the property, you simply need to have your agent draft *Cancellation Instructions* and submit those to escrow and the Seller. Once the Cancellation Instructions have been signed by all parties, any monies you have on deposit with escrow will be returned, according to the terms of the PSA.

If you decide you want to purchase the property and do not have any credit requests, you simply need to send an executed *Contingency Removal* to the Seller and escrow letting them know you'll be moving forward under the terms of the PSA. This is a document that your agent or escrow can prepare for you to sign.

If you've decided you want the property, but have discovered some things that require a credit or price reduction, you may request this from the Seller. Oftentimes, this request is combined with the Contingency Removal to strengthen your negotiating position. What usually occurs is your agent drafts a letter to the Seller itemizing the total credit you request, as well as a detailed explanation. At the end of the letter, you stipulate that upon mutual acceptance of these new terms and price, you, the Buyer, are prepared to move forward, remove your books/records and physical inspection contingency, and have your deposit go "hard," or non-refundable. What this means to the Seller is that if he agrees to your credit request, he has a deal and your deposit will become non-refundable. So, if for some reason you don't perform and close escrow, you forfeit your deposit to the Seller and he's able to remarket the property to a new Buyer.

I've often felt that combining your credit request with your Contingency Removal is the most powerful approach to achieve your goal. It basically lets the Seller know two things: That you're serious about purchasing the property and are prepared to have your deposit go hard and become non-refundable, but only if your credit request is granted. The Seller now has a decision to make; and if he agrees to your request, the deal moves ahead.

Note that every locale has its own customs and ways of doing business and some areas are far more laid back than others. Larger cities such as New York and Los Angeles often have a more aggressive approach to deal making and Sellers expect more of Buyers. This usually means larger deposits (3% of the purchase price, or more), shorter DD periods, and non-refundability of deposits upon removal of contingencies.

Step 9: Loan Application (Financing Contingency) - Typically in a PSA, the Buyer is afforded multiple contingencies during the transaction. The first two are the *Physical Inspection* and *Books & Records* contingencies discussed above. This consumes the bulk of your time during the DD period. The third is your *Title Contingency* which allows the Buyer to verify title on the property. This is one of the items you addressed during your DD period as well. Usually, the Physical Inspection, Books & Records, and Title Contingencies run for the same length of time (10 days, 14 days, etc.) and begin and expire at the same time.

The final contingency deals with your *Financing*, or loan. This Contingency period begins at the same time as the others—the Effective Date of the contract—but may run longer than the others. In many cases, it may run for 21-45 days, or until the loan is approved. It depends on the product type, geographic location, and local custom. For example, in southern California, it's typical in the multi-family market for Buyers to make offers with very short DD periods (7-10 days) and NO financing contingencies, which means that if they can't obtain a loan once they've removed contingencies, they either forfeit their deposit or purchase the property on an all-cash basis. In other areas, such as Texas, the financing contingency often remains in place until the Buyer has obtained loan approval. In a case like this, the Buyer doesn't run the risk of forfeiting his deposit if he is unable to obtain financing. Obviously, the longer the financing contingency, the better this is. Ideally, you'd like the Seller to allow the financing contingency to remain in place until you received loan approval, but this doesn't always happen.

During your DD period, you want to provide the lender that gave you the initial loan quote with as much information on the property as possible so they can get the lending process started and determine with a high degree of certainty, that financing is available and at what rate and terms. Since you're not paying all cash, the loan is crucial to the successful purchase of the property. You won't usually submit a loan application fee until you've removed all of your contingencies (except Financing) and are certain you're going to go forward with the purchase–because this fee is generally non-refundable. Oftentimes, the cost for the loan application fee will be a few thousand dollars, plus another few thousand dollars for your appraisal.

Your Financing Contingency often runs for a set period of time (14 days or 30 days) and may expire before you receive loan approval. This means that sometimes you're required to remove your Financing Contingency before you have loan approval and know with 100% certainty that you can obtain a loan at a rate and terms acceptable to you. If this is your situation, you want to speak with the lender and make sure you understand what potential pitfalls, if any, remain so that when you do remove this final contingency, you're making the best decision. An alternative may be to request an extension of your Financing Contingency from the Seller. He may be receptive if you can provide him with a letter from the lender showing proof that you've submitted an application and detailing how much time you need. Additionally, you might offer to increase your deposit with escrow in return for an extension. It all depends on how friendly your Seller is and how much confidence he has in your ability to perform.

If your Financing Contingency expires at the same time as your other Contingencies—meaning they all run for the same length of time—when you go to remove your contingencies, you remove this one as well. At that time, your deposit becomes non-refundable, and sometimes, if called for in the PSA, is released to the Seller. If your Financing Contingency extends past the others (i.e., 45 days vs. 14 days), when you remove your other Contingencies, you still have this one left. While language varies from one PSA to the next, your Financing Contingency typically provides that if you make all reasonable attempts to obtain financing within a certain time frame and are unable to, you may cancel the transaction and your deposit is returned.

In my career, I've seen very few deals fall apart due to financing after all other contingencies have been removed. If you're diligent during the process and get the lender what they need, you should be okay. Just remember, exceptions to every rule can always occur.

Step 10: Loan Funds/Close of Escrow – Once the lender completes the underwriting process, you receive Loan Approval which means your loan has been approved and you're able to close the deal. The lender has you go to their office or to escrow to sign all loan documents. There are probably 50 pages or more of paperwork, and sometimes 150 pages or more—usually on Commercial Mortgage Backed Securitized (CMBS) loans. Once the documents are signed, you wire your balance of funds due to escrow, and the lender "funds the loan" and wires in the total loan amount you were approved for. The amount you need to wire is calculated by subtracting the total property cost less your initial deposit and the loan proceeds due from the lender. This figure includes title and escrow fees, as well as other fees that you'll be charged to purchase the property.

Once the loan funds and all monies are received by title or escrow, the sale is recorded with the local Assessor's Office and title is officially transferred to you. Congratulations! You're now the owner of an income-generating property.

Step 11: Take-over of Property/Management – Once you take title and possession of the property, one of the first things you need to do is convert all utilities into your name to make sure water, power, and gas are not turned off to the property or the tenants. You also need to decide how you're going to manage the property: Either by yourself or with the help of a professional management company. A general rule of thumb is that once you have 9 or more units, it becomes cost- and time-effective to engage the services of a professional manager. Additionally, you should consult with your agent regarding local laws requiring onsite management based on how many units the property has (this is usually only a requirement for multi-family property). For example, any property in Los Angeles County containing 16 units or more requires an on-site manager by law.

The process outlined in the above steps can be time-consuming and at times frustrating. It can take anywhere from 30 to 90 days or more, from the time you submit your first offer, until you fund your loan and take title. Duplexes and fourplexes take less time as they're usually purchased with single-family residential loans, while 5(+)-unit multi-family properties, as well as all other commercial properties, are purchased with commercial loans that typically take a minimum of 45 days to underwrite and fund. My best suggestion is to be prepared for the unexpected. It's best to give the lender all the information they request as soon as possible to keep the process moving. As the purchase price increases, the deal complexity usually does as well. Make sure you surround yourself with competent sales agents/brokers and lenders. They'll help you navigate the transaction and avoid unexpected pitfalls.

CHAPTER 7 — LEVERAGE:
THE GOOD, THE BAD AND THE UGLY - EVERYTHING YOU NEED TO KNOW ABOUT GETTING A LOAN

This chapter is divided into smaller parts and designed to help you understand what types of loans are available, the lending process, and how loans can affect your investment decision. Each part builds on the previous one; and at the end of this chapter, you should feel very comfortable with the lending process.

At the time I started writing this book in summer 2007, we were at the beginning of the sub-prime lending meltdown. Much has occurred since then, and many of the lessons learned during that time are included in this book. The meltdown started as the number of delinquent loans issued to sub-prime borrowers began to jump. In fact, in Los Angeles County, the number of foreclosures in 2007 was up over 800% year-over-year. The increased foreclosure rate began to cause problems for companies like Countrywide and Ameriquest Mortgage, and would lead to the bankruptcy and disbanding of some of the largest mortgage lenders in the country (Ameriquest is out of business and Countrywide was purchased by Bank of America).

Lenders and loans are almost always at the heart of any real estate transaction. That's because you very rarely see a property purchased with all cash. You may see a buyer put as much as 40%-50% down, or more, but it's rare to see a buyer put down the entire amount. As discussed in earlier chapters, it just doesn't make sense in most cases. One of the great benefits of real estate over other investments is the ability to use *Other People's Money* (OPM, as you may have heard it referred to elsewhere). And for most of the time period from 2001-2006, it was very easy to borrow money; and in some cases, too easy.

On the SFR level, lenders were handing out 100% LTV loans, and sometimes even covering closing costs on top of that; so borrowers literally had $0 invested in a property. Often, these loans could be obtained using a *Stated Income* application which meant that you didn't need to provide any documentation supporting the income you reported on your application. As long as your credit was good, you could get a loan. And, if your credit wasn't good, there were still many lenders lining up to work with you.

Banks divvy borrowers up into different categories based on their credit scores (FICO), ranging from A or Prime to Alt-A to Sub-prime, with Prime being A credit or excellent and Sub-prime usually representing a 620 FICO score or lower. The risk of default increases as you move from an A borrower to a Sub-Prime borrower, and lenders compensate for this by charging borrowers higher interest rates and loan origination fees.

Very loose lending guidelines and rapidly increasing home values across the United States came to a head in early 2007, as foreclosure rates around the country began to climb. This was largely due to borrowers' ARMs (Adjustable Rate Mortgages) resetting in a higher interest rate environment. After all, the 3- or 5-year fixed ARM that a borrower took in 2001-2004, was adjusting for the first time in 2007. The Prime Rate had jumped over 4%; and all of a sudden, people's monthly mortgage payments were increasing by hundreds, if not thousands, of dollars and many were unable to afford the increased payments. At the same time, home values were starting to stabilize and fall; and markets were saturated with homes for sale, causing houses to sit for 6 months or more in many markets. Homeowners were no longer able to sell their homes for more than they paid and did not have the option of selling to stave off foreclosure.

This meltdown had a huge ripple effect throughout the lending industry, affecting lenders such as Countrywide and Ameriquest on home loans, as well as J.P. Morgan and others on CMBS and Life Company loans. First, it forced residential lenders to toughen their lending guidelines and make it more difficult for the average borrower to get a loan. Second, it created a liquidity issue in the secondary markets for many of the loans that were being sold, and it forced lenders to increase their spreads to compensate for the perceived risks they were taking by buying these loans.

Now I know all of this sounds pretty complicated, but it all boils down to this: August 2007 brought tougher lending guidelines and higher spreads on loans, making it harder and more expensive to buy real estate. And my guess is that moving forward, the heydays of 2002-2006 are over; and we may never see as lax a lending environment as we did then. So, it's more important than ever to properly account for financing in your investment decision and make sure you fully understand the ramifications of the loan you're considering and what options are available.

PART I: HOW TO GET A LOAN:
Who funds them, how much does it cost, what type do you want (prepay penalties, fixed vs. variable, etc.).

Getting a loan. The first step in the loan application process is to speak with your lender or mortgage broker about the property you want to buy. You can obtain a loan one of two ways: From a direct lender such as Wells Fargo or Bank of America, or with the aid of a mortgage broker. Both options have their advantages.

Mortgage brokers usually charge a 1% origination fee (of the loan amount) for their services. This means that on a $3MM loan you'll incur a $30,000 fee that is paid to your mortgage broker, in addition to the other fees such as appraisal, application/origination fees, and other third-party reports. This cost can sometimes be circumvented if you apply directly to the lender making the loan, such as Wells Fargo or Bank of America. The advantage you gain by using the broker is that, oftentimes, you're unaware of who the local lenders are in your area that will be interested in your loan request (and many do not deal directly with the public and only work through a broker network). Further, your mortgage broker will help you package the deal to make it as appealing as possible to the lender, thereby increasing your odds of getting maximum loan proceeds at the most competitive rate.

My suggestion for many of my clients is to use the services of a mortgage broker unless they have a "plain vanilla" deal they know they can take directly to a lender. Less complicated apartment deals are often good candidates for direct lenders, while larger deals with loan amounts over $3MM or more are better candidates for a mortgage broker. For most CMBS and Life Company (LC) loans, you will almost always need to use the services of a broker. These are more complicated transactions involving large Wall Street institutions and require the assistance of a trained professional to help you organize your loan package into a "book" that can be shopped/marketed to various lenders. A "book" is a loan package that your broker creates that contains all the information on the deal including pricing, location, P&L info, sales and rental comparables, and anything else the mortgage broker thinks is relevant for the lender to review.

The key factors in any loan are the interest rate, fixed-rate period, prepayment penalty, amortization period, and the loan amount itself.

Each of these factors plays an important role in your loan and how much your payments are going to be each month. Since your cash-on-cash return is directly tied to the amount of the debt service payment you make each month, it's important to understand each factor and how it impacts your loan.

Who funds loans? Loans can be made by a variety of institutions beginning with your local neighborhood bank, all the way to Wall Street institutions such as Lehman Brothers and Pension Funds such as CALPERS. Local banks typically fund what are known as *Conventional Loans*, and include Wells Fargo, Bank of America, Washington Mutual, and any local Savings & Loan. The loans made by these banks may be Adjustable Rate Mortgages (fixed for 3-12 months) or 3-, 5-, and 7-year fixed loans with some type of graduated prepayment penalty.

Wall Street lenders fund what are known as CMBS or *conduit loans*. CMBS is an acronym for Commercial Mortgage Backed Securitized loans, and these were created in the late 1990s as a way for Wall Street investors to get involved in the real estate markets. These loans are usually fixed for 10 years and carry steep prepayment penalties in the form of defeasance (discussed later in this Chapter). These loans have strict underwriting guidelines and are usually sold in the secondary market shortly after being originated. They're costly to originate and total loan fees can equal 2% or more of the loan amount. On a $10MM loan, it's not unusual for a borrower to spend $200,000 or more on loan origination fees, third-party reports, and attorney fees. The minimum loan amount on a CMBS is usually $5MM and up; but as of late, some CMBS lenders have begun to offer "small CMBS" programs for loans of $1MM and more. The fees on these programs have been capped, making it more affordable for the small investor. CMBS lenders like to loan on well-located properties with good credit tenants.

Another source of lending money is the Life Companies, or LCs. These are usually comprised of pension and life insurance companies looking for a safe place to invest their money. They're only looking for a modest return on their investment; and real estate provides them with a secure way to earn it. Like CMBS loans, these are usually fixed for 10 years and carry steep prepayment penalties, typically in the form of yield-maintenance (discussed later in this Chapter). They're somewhat easier to originate and not as costly as CMBS loans. LCs usually require a minimum loan amount of $3-5MM and up, in addition to a well-located property with good credit tenants.

Loan Term. Loan rates can be fixed from 1 month to 10 years or more. Conventional lenders usually offer a 1-, 3-, 5-, 7- and 10-year fixed program, while CMBS and LC lenders usually only offer a 10-year fixed program, with some now considering 5-year fixed terms on a deal-by-deal basis.

At the time you originate your loan, you have to decide how long you'd like the interest rate to be fixed. Most borrowers choose among 3-, 5-, 7-, or 10-year fixed terms. Your goal is to try to match the length of the loan with your anticipated hold period. For example, if you think you're going to hold a property for 2-4 years, you want to take a 3- or 5-year fixed loan term. If you think you're going to hold a property for 7 years or longer, you want to take a 10-year fixed loan term. The only time you might want to go with a 1-year ARM is if you plan on flipping the property and selling quickly, or you believe rates are going to fall and you plan on doing a refinance in the near future.

As you might guess, banks charge a higher rate of interest as the fixed-rate term increases. The difference in rate might be 6.5% on a 3-year fixed and 7.125% on a 10-year fixed. You want to check with your lender to see what pricing is currently available, but typically, the rate will increase the longer it's fixed.

There are rare occasions where this is not true, such as periods during 2007, when the debt markets believed that short-term debt was pricier than long-term debt. This occurs when rates on the 10-year Treasury bond are lower than the 1- and 5-year Treasury bond. This simply means that Wall Street believes debt is more expensive in the near-term, but will become cheaper in the future. In these rare instances, you find the pricing on a 10-year fixed to be very competitive with a 3- and 5-year fixed. In these cases, I suggest going with a longer-term fixed rate, assuming the prepayment penalty is reasonable and will not be an impediment to any future disposition plans you may have for the property.

Interest Rates and Spreads. One of the key factors in a loan is your interest rate. Your goal is to secure the lowest interest rate for the longest period of time. To do this, you need to understand how banks determine interest rates and underlying spreads. An interest rate is usually comprised of an index plus margin (or spread). An index is the base rate from which your interest rate will be calculated. Popular indices include LIBOR, Prime, and the 10-Year Treasury. The margin is the amount the lender adds to the index to arrive at the rate of interest being charged. For example, many home loans are priced as "Prime + pricing." This means that you add the margin to the prevailing Prime Rate to arrive at the interest rate.

$$Rate = Index + Margin \text{ (or Spread)}$$

$$Rate = Prime\ Rate + 2.00\%$$

In the example above, the margin is equal to 2.00%. This means that if the prevailing Prime Rate at the time of loan origination was 4.00%, the total interest rate charged to the borrower would be 6.00%, calculated as follows:

$$6.00\% = 4.00\% + 2.00\%$$

Oftentimes, the margin (or spread) is expressed in basis points or bps (pronounced "bips") — 1.00% equals 100 bps; and a margin of 2.00% is equal to 200 bps or 200 bips.

Conventional loans are generally tied to Prime, COFI (Cost of Funds Index) or LIBOR, with LIBOR being the most popular. LIBOR (London Inter-Bank Offered Rate), mentioned earlier, is the most common benchmark used as it stays relatively stable over time, which is very important if you have a loan tied to it. The margin on Conventional Loans has run between 2.5%-2.875% the past several years (2001-2007). Since most lenders tie their rates to the same index, it's important for you to understand the margin they use. The higher the margin, the higher your interest rate will be; so pay attention to this figure.

CMBS and LC loans are typically tied to the 10-Year Treasury. The margin on these loans is usually referred to as the spread, and can vary from 110-225 bps or more, depending on the quality of the underlying real estate and tenant. In August 2007, the spreads being charged by lenders jumped considerably after the lending crisis occurred, and went from an average of 80-110 bps on prime property to 150-180 bps, basically doubling overnight. Since the beginning of 2008, spreads have increased even further, going as high as 235-350 bps. The greater the perceived risk by the lender, the higher the spread they charge to compensate for that risk.

For example, the rate on a loan on a McDonald's located in the heart of Los Angeles will be far lower than the rate on a small strip center in the middle of Kansas with no credit tenants. The reason for this is the default risk with the McDonald's is far less than with the strip center, and the tenant is far stronger financially if something were to happen. Usually, large tenants like McDonald's or Rite Aid have a corporate guarantee on the lease that stipulates if the tenant goes "dark" (out of business) the monthly lease payments will still be made. This is not usually the case with a smaller Mom & Pop tenant who does not have strong financials or the ability to continuing paying their lease if their business goes belly up.

Adjustability. CMBS and LC loans are always fixed and never adjust, unlike many conventional loans. These loans are due and payable at the end of their initial 10-year terms; and once that time is up, the lender expects their money back. At this point, the borrower has a few options available: Pay off the loan with fresh Capital (i.e., cash sitting in a bank account); refinance the current loan with a new loan using the proceeds from the refinance to pay off the current loan; or sell the property and use the proceeds from the sale to pay off the current loan.

Unlike a CMBS or LC loan that never adjusts and must be paid back at the end of the loan term, there's sometimes another option available on a Conventional Loan at the end of the fixed-rate period. While they're due and payable *sometimes*, other times the rate adjusts periodically and the lender continues with the loan. For example, a 3-year ARM might be fixed at 6.0% for 3 years, and then adjust every 6 months at the beginning of Year 3. In this case, the lender is not requiring the loan be paid off, but rather continues to extend the loan to the borrower with regular adjustments to the interest rate.

For example, if you originated a loan in 2004, the rate might have been calculated as follows:

Step 1: Rate = Index + Margin

Step 2: Rate = LIBOR + 2.875%

Step 3: Rate = 3.125% + 2.875%

Step 4: Rate = 6.00%

At the end of the primary term (sometime in 2007, 3 years later), your rate would adjust according to the terms agreed to at the time of origination and stipulated in the loan documents. Typically, ARMs adjust every 6-12 months, with a *floor* and a *ceiling* on how much they can move up or down in any one adjustment period and over the life of the loan. The specifics of your loan are spelled out in the Commitment Letter you receive at time of your application, as well as in the loan documents you sign at the time of closing. It's very important to read through these documents carefully and make sure they reflect the understanding and agreement you have with the lender. It's not uncommon for an error to occur when these documents are being drafted or "drawn;" so make sure you have someone who understands these documents review them before you sign.

Once your primary term has expired and your rate begins to adjust, you want to understand how often and how much it can move. Your loan documents clearly define this information. The ceiling and floor on the adjustment mean just what they say. The ceiling is the maximum the rate can increase to and the floor is the minimum. Typically, the ceiling is 5%-6% higher than your start rate (the rate your loan was originated at—in this example 6%), and the floor is typically your start rate or, possibly, 1% less (in this example either 6% or 5%). In addition to your floor and ceiling, there's a maximum amount your rate can adjust during any one period. Usually, this is fixed at 2%. So, if at the end of Year 3 LIBOR has moved from 3.125% up to 6.125%, your loan would adjust as follows:

$$Rate = Index + Margin$$

$$Rate = 6.125\% + 2.875\%$$

$$Rate = 9.00\%$$

However, if the maximum your rate can adjust is fixed at 2% in any one period; your rate would move from 6.00% to 8.00%, not 9.00%. During the next adjustment period, it may continue to move upward if the index your rate is tied to is still high. As your rate adjusts, so will your mortgage or debt service payment; and it's important to be prepared for these adjustments as they can have a great impact on your cash-flow (more on this in Chapters 8 & 9). Many borrowers find that it's a good time to consider a refinance once their rate begins to adjust upwards.

Interest-Only Payments. Within the past few years, lenders have begun to allow borrowers to make interest-only payments during some or all of the loan's term. This means that the payment you make each month is only to service the debt you've borrowed and does not go towards reducing, or "paying down," the principal borrowed. The advantage of an interest-only payment is that it's lower than a fully-amortized payment and, therefore, increases your cash-on-cash return, or your spendable income. This has become a widely popular component of most loans and is appealing to many investors, especially those who plan to hold a property five years or less and seek cash flow. CMBS and LC lenders have been known to originate loans with as many as ten years of I/O (Interest-Only) payments, while conventional lenders usually offer no more than five. Since the lending crisis began in August 2007, lenders have pulled back some on their willingness to extend I/O on loans; so, make sure you shop around if this is an important feature to you.

Prepayment Penalties. Most loans come with prepayment penalties. This is a penalty paid to the lender for paying back, or retiring, a loan early or before the expiration of the fixed-rate period. On a CMBS or LC loan, this would constitute payment before the end of the 10-year term; and on a Conventional Loan, it might be paying off a loan in Year 2 of a 5-Year fixed-term loan. Prepayment penalties can be negotiated at the time of application, but you'll have little success changing the terms with a CMBS or LC lender. Conventional lenders, however, are more lenient; and this is a point you should discuss with them. Depending on the lending environment and how aggressive the lenders are, you might be able to secure a loan with no prepayment penalty at all. Your goal is to try and get the smallest prepayment penalty for the shortest period of time.

The prepayment penalty from a conventional lender typically steps down over time, being largest in Year 1 and gradually declining to zero over time. On a 5-year fixed, you might see a 5-4-3-2-1 prepayment penalty which means that in Year 1, you have a 5% prepayment penalty, 3% in Year 2, and down to 1% in Year 5. That means that if you were to pay the loan off early in Year 3, you would owe the bank a penalty equal to 3% of the loan amount. On a $1MM loan, you'd owe a $30,000 prepayment penalty.

When you originate your loan, it's important to understand what the prepayment penalty is and how it will affect your future decision-making about the property you're buying. A large prepayment penalty (as we see below) can drastically affect your ability to sell a property in the future.

CMBS and LC lenders have steep prepayment penalties that encourage the borrower to keep the loan for the full term. CMBS lenders use what is called *defeasance*. It's a difficult figure to calculate, but typically equals 10% of the loan amount. On a $10MM loan, your prepayment penalty, or defeasance, might equal as much as $1MM. There are many websites devoted to defeasance that can calculate the amount you'd owe. One that I've used with success is http://www.defeasewithease.com. You need your loan amount, interest rate, amortization period, and a few other items pertinent to your loan to do the calculation.

LC lenders use yield-maintenance to calculate their prepayment penalties. Yield-maintenance is similar to defeasance and almost as costly. It's calculated using a complicated formula that takes into account the difference between the interest rate of the loan and the prevailing interest rate in the market: The larger the difference between the two, the larger the prepayment penalty. As with CMBS lenders, these figures are typically steep and can range from 5%-9% or more of the loan amount. There are various calculators you can visit on the Internet to approximate what the penalty would be; and you're also encouraged to speak with your lender's Prepayment Department to get an exact figure.

The key to understanding a yield-maintenance prepayment penalty is the fact that if the prevailing interest rate in the market place is roughly 125-150 bps higher than the interest rate of the loan, the prepayment penalty may fall to zero. For example, if you have a 10-year fixed at 6.0% that you originated in 2004, and the interest rate for a 10-year fixed in 2008 was 7.5%, your prepayment penalty would be close to $0. This is because the calculation is largely based on the difference between the rates. As rates move higher, your prepayment penalty goes down. Lenders are happy to have you prepay their money that they lent you at 6.0% so they can re-lend it to someone else at 7.5% and earn a higher rate of return.

Prepayment penalties are always going to be least financially intrusive with conventional loans, and that's one of their main advantages. CMBS and LC companies are notorious for their aggressive prepayment penalties and the financial binds borrowers have found themselves in as a result. It's difficult to completely predict the future; and if you do find yourself forced to sell an asset that has a CMBS or LC loan, you might be faced with steep and unforeseen prepayment penalties. These can significantly eat into your profits and even result in a loss. You always want to make sure that the benefits of the CMBS or LC loan outweigh their negatives when you make the decision to go with one. The biggest benefit of the CMBS/LC loans is that the interest rates are usually 25-50 bps lower than on a corresponding conventional loan. On a $5MM loan this could equal $12,500-$25,000 a year in interest expense savings, or $125,000-$250,000 in savings over a 10-year term.

Amortization periods. Another component of your loan that affects your monthly payments is the amortization period. This is the length of time the lender gives you to repay the principal borrowed. Amortization periods range from 20 to 35 years, with most falling at either 25 or 30 years. Multi-family properties generally have loans underwritten against a 30-year amortization, while commercial properties vary in amortization periods depending upon the age of the property, the location, and credit of the tenant(s).

A client of mine purchased a single-tenant NNN National drugstore and was able to get a 35-year amortization period, which is uncommon, but not unheard of. You should expect a 20- to 30-year amortization for a typical commercial property; and this is a point that *can* be negotiated with the lender. Some multi-family lenders increased the amortization periods to as many as 40 years in 2006, as they tried to compete aggressively for new business. Recently, however, banks have pulled these offerings back in an effort to tighten underwriting guidelines.

The longer the amortization period, the lower your monthly payment is since you have more years to repay the principal you borrowed. This can be quite helpful if you need/want to increase your monthly cash flow and cash-on-cash return. However, remember that the longer your loan is amortized, the more interest you pay on the borrowed money over the life of the loan. Less of your monthly payment goes towards principal reduction and more towards interest. The good news is that interest expense is tax deductible, which saves you money.

Investors looking to purchase a deal they're going to hold for 3-5 years or less should push for the longest amortization period the lender will consider. If you plan to hold the building long-term, meaning 10 years or more, stick with a more traditional amortization period of 25 to 30 years with a goal to pay the loan off.

Loan Assumability. Assumability refers to whether or not the loan you have can be assumed by another borrower. Not all loans are assumable, but most are. Typically, the lender requires the new borrower to submit a full loan package to be reviewed by their underwriters. The lender is more than likely going to conduct a building inspection and possibly an appraisal. The total cost to assume a loan is usually one point (1%) of the current loan amount; so, on a $5MM loan, it would cost $50,000 for the assumption. These fees are usually paid by the new borrower assuming the loan; but this can be negotiated between the Buyer and Seller.

When you first originate your loan, your Commitment Letter from the lender addresses whether your loan is assumable and under what terms. This information is also included in your loan documents, and you should review this item carefully. A lender that allows your loan to be assumed provides you with one more option when you go to sell your property. After all, if you've got a loan with a great rate fixed for a number of years, it may prove attractive to the next purchaser and enhance the sale of the property either in the form of less time on the market or a higher price, or both.

Many loans originated during 2003-2005, carried very low interest rates. In fact, some of the CMBS loans have rates that were fixed as low as 5.0% for 10 years and are very attractive candidates for assumption since the next owner greatly benefits from such a low rate as it's far below the current rate offered in the market. The negative, if there is one in an assumption like this, is that typically, when you do an assumption, you *do not* achieve maximum leverage on a property.

For example, someone who purchased a $3MM retail center in 2003, might have been required to put 25% down; so, they originated a $2.25MM loan (75% LTV). When that investor goes to sell his property in 2007, he might ask $4MM for the deal. Since the loan he has is a 10-year fixed (with 6 years left) at 5.0% for $2.25MM, the new owner would be required to put down $1.75MM, or 44% down (56% LTV). If the new Buyer were to go out into the debt markets to look for a new loan, the lender might require 30-35% down, allowing him/her to get better leverage, but at a much higher rate, most likely 6.5% instead of 5.0%. Therefore, the new Buyer has a decision to make based on how much Capital he has available for a down payment, and how important leverage and cash flow are.

In the past few years, I've seen more properties for sale that have assumable financing that a new Buyer might find attractive. It's always a trade-off between leverage, interest rate, and length of the fixed-rate term. After all, since the loan was originated some years back, there's usually only 3-6 years left on the fixed-rate term. Depending upon your anticipated hold period, this could be a positive or negative. It's a positive if you're assuming a low- interest rate loan and only plan to hold the property for a few more years. It may be a negative if you're a long-term holder and are going to have to refinance the loan in a few years at what you predict will be a higher interest rate.

Leverage is more important to some investors than others. Some investors, particularly those in a 1031 Exchange, might need slightly higher leverage so they can conform to the guidelines of a 1031 Exchange and satisfy both the debt and equity requirements of their exchange.

As you can see, there are many factors involved in a loan; and it's important to understand them all. Certain loans are better at providing leverage and assumability, while others have better prepayment and I/O (Interest-Only) options. Many of my clients who originate loans of $3MM or less, typically focus on local banks and conventional loans. Clients looking for loans of $3MM and up, usually focus on LC and

CMBS loans as they favor the lower rate they usually offer, as well as the extended years of I/O. The major trade-off with an LC or CMBS loan over a conventional loan is acceptance of the stiff prepayment penalty in the form of yield-maintenance or defeasance, as well as the rigorous and very expensive application process.

Here is a list that summarizes the pros and cons of each loan type.

	Conventional	LC/CMBS
Application Process	Easy	Difficult
Application Fees	Reasonable	Expensive
Interest Rate	Average	Excellent
Leverage	Average-Good	Good-Excellent
Assumability	Good	Good-Excellent
I/O Period	Good	Good-Excellent
Prepayment Penalty	Good	Expensive
Loan Size	Up to $8-10MM	$3-5MM & up
Amortization Period	Good	Good-Excellent
Loan Term	1-10 year fixed	5-10 year fixed

PART II: HOW DOES A LENDER CALCULATE HOW MUCH TO LEND YOU? - DCRs, Etc.

When you approach a lender for a loan, one of the most important things you want to know is how much money they're willing to lend you. Leverage can make or break most deals; and if you can't get a large enough loan, you might be forced to pass on a great opportunity since most investors only have so much money available for a down payment

Lenders use DCRs (or DSCRs) to calculate how large a loan they're prepared to lend on a deal. DCR is short for Debt Coverage Ratio and DSCR for Debt Service Coverage Ratio. They mean and refer to the same thing and are used interchangeably by lending institutions. This is the single most important figure used during the underwriting process, and one I believe every investor should understand intimately and be able to calculate comfortably. In laymen's terms, the DCR is simply the ratio of your Net Operating Income (NOI) divided by your Debt Service (DS) or Mortgage Payment. Expressed in mathematical terms, it's simply:

$$DCR = NOI/DS$$

Lenders generally like to see a deal with a minimum of a 1.15-1.20 DCR. This means that your NOI is 1.15-1.20 times greater than your Debt Service payments, or 115-120% greater. What this really means is that the income your property generates after all expenses are paid—your NOI—is greater than the mortgage payment you're required to make each month. And, after you pay all your expenses and your mortgage, you'll have a profit each month. Lenders want to see a 1.15 minimum DCR because they want to make sure you earn a profit and that there's a buffer left over after you pay your mortgage so that if something unexpected occurs, you won't go broke.

To calculate the DCR, the lender needs to figure out the DS and NOI figures. First, they calculate the property's NOI based on their internal underwriting guidelines. They take the building's income and subtract reasonable expenses based on local custom. It's important to note that in Los Angeles County, the local apartment vacancy rate averages 3%; however, lenders in the area use a 5% rate when calculating their NOIs. This means that the lender's NOI will be lower than yours since they discount the GSI by a larger number for vacancy loss. Lenders also include a budget in their NOI calculation for repairs and maintenance; so, it's important for you to speak with your lender to understand how they arrive at their NOI figure. Every dollar of NOI lost will cost you in the total loan amount the lender is willing to offer.

Once the lender calculates their projected NOI for the property, they determine what DCR they are prepared to lend at. The DCR varies based on product type (residential vs. commercial vs. office), as well as geographical location and other factors. This is a figure you can and should discuss with your lender, and it *is* negotiable. If your contact at the lender cannot lower the DCR they're willing to underwrite against, you can request that his manager review the file and grant an "exception." Remember, the lower the DCR, the better the leverage you obtain. And while not everyone looks for a maximum LTV loan, it's good to know that if you need to borrow more loan dollars, they're available to you.

Once the lender calculates the NOI and settles on a DCR, they have two pieces of the puzzle to calculate the final component: The DS, or Debt Service. By dividing the NOI by the DCR, you can find the maximum DS the property's cash flow can support.

$$DS = NOI/DCR$$

The DS is calculated using a somewhat complicated formula based on the following components: Loan amount, interest rate (sometimes called the "qualifying rate"), and amortization period. Using these components you can arrive at what the fully-amortized annual loan payment would be.

The purpose of these calculations and the DCR is to find out how large a loan the lender is willing to make. From the beginning of your discussions with a lender, some of the important points you discuss include the amortization period and interest rate. Since you'll know these two figures, you're able to use them to calculate the loan amount the bank is willing to lend. By working backwards with a financial calculator or in Excel, you can use the DS figure, amortization period, and interest rate to calculate the loan amount. This amount will be the maximum loan the bank will allow you to borrow.

If the lender comes back with the loan amount they're willing to offer and you are unhappy with it, wishing it were higher, you'll need to convince the lender to do one of the following: Lower their interest rate, increase their amortization period, lower their DCR, or increase the NOI they calculated for the property. By changing any one of those figures, you can effectively increase the loan amount the property can support. For example, some lenders include a very high management fee in their underwriting. If you can convince the lender that you'll be able to competently manage the property for less money, you'll be able to increase the NOI and, therefore, the loan amount.

For those of you who enjoy math and want to calculate these figures yourself, I've provided the formula below. When using Microsoft Excel, you want to use the PMT formula to calculate the fully amortized monthly debt service payment. The formula is as follows:

$$=-PMT(I8/12,360,I7,0)*12$$

This formula asks you for the interest rate (cell I8 in this example, but will change based the cell location in your worksheet), loan amount (cell I7 in this example), and amortization period (360 months - NOT years); and will automatically calculate the payment on a fully amortized loan. By doing this in Excel, you can change any one of the variables provided and your monthly payment will change as well. If you're working with an Interest-Only (I/O) Loan, you'll want to use the following formula:

$$=-(I8*I7)/12$$

In this case, the loan payment is derived by multiplying the loan amount times the interest rate and dividing by 12 months.

Remember, the lender tells you what the interest rate and amortization period are. They also tell you what the NOI and DCR are; so, the only variable you solve for is the loan amount. Your goal when underwriting a deal is to get a realistic idea of how large a loan the current NOI can support. This will lead you to your LTV and cash-on-cash return. A final note: Lenders will also use a fully-amortized payment when calculating the maximum loan amount a property's NOI can support, not an I/O payment.

PART III: LEVERAGE AS YOUR FRIEND AND FOE.

Leverage can be both good and bad. There are/were loans available for residential property where you could put down as little as 0%; and there are loans on commercial property that allow you to put down as little as 2%-3%. In both scenarios, the borrower finds himself in a highly leveraged situation with little equity in the deal, and with a very large monthly debt service payment. Sometimes this is good; and other times it can be catastrophic.

When people talk about leverage they sometimes refer to positive and negative leverage. Positive leverage occurs when the difference between the CAP rate of your investment and the interest rate at which you borrow funds to finance that investment is positive, or greater than 0. This means that if you buy a 7.0% CAP property and you borrow money at 6.0%, you have positive leverage. Since the spread between the CAP and the interest rate is greater than 0 and positive, you earn a rate of return higher than 7.0%. Remember, the CAP rate on any deal is the rate of return you would earn if you were to purchase the property all cash. So a 7.0% CAP deal would have a 7.0% cash-on-cash return if you were to buy it all cash (no debt). Intuitively, this should make sense. If you borrow money from one friend at 6.0% and lend it another friend at 7.0%, you are going to earn a small return on every dollar.

As you know by now, most people do not buy real estate all cash. It just doesn't make sense. The beauty of real estate is the ability to use debt (or Other People's Money) to pay for it. Your goal, however, is to put yourself into a positive leverage situation as often as possible. You always want to make sure that the CAP rate on the property is HIGHER than the interest rate on the debt. If it's not, you're going to end up with negative leverage. The examples below will clearly outline the difference.

Example 1: Positive Leverage - 7.0% CAP vs. 5.5% Interest Rate

Purchase Price	$1,000,000
Cap Rate:	7.0%
NOI	$70,000
LTV:	75.0%
Loan Amount	$750,000
Interest Rate on Debt:	5.5%
Fully Amortized Loan Payment	$51,101
Interest Only (I/O) Loan Payment	$41,250
Pre-Tax Cash Flow (fully amortized loan payment)	$18,899
Cash-on-cash return (fully amortized loan payment):	**7.5%**
Pre-Tax Cash Flow (I/O loan payment)	$28,750
Cash-on-cash return (I/O loan payment):	11.4%

Example 2: Negative Leverage - 6.0% CAP vs. 6.5% Interest Rate

Purchase Price	$1,000,000
Cap Rate:	6.0%
NOI	$60,000
LTV:	75.0%
Loan Amount	$750,000
Interest Rate on Debt:	6.5%
Fully Amortized Loan Payment	$56,886
Interest Only (I/O) Loan Payment	$48,750
Pre-Tax Cash Flow (fully amortized loan payment)	$3,114
Cash-on-cash return (fully amortized loan payment):	1.1%
Pre-Tax Cash Flow (I/O loan payment)	$11,250
Cash-on-cash return (I/O loan payment):	4.4%

In Example 1, the borrower is positively leveraged, so the cash-on-cash return is greater than the CAP rate of the deal (7.5% is larger than 7.0% for the fully-amortized payment). It's important to note that in order to obtain positive leverage on a fully-amortized loan you need approximately a 1.4% spread (or 140 bps) between the CAP rate and Interest rate. If you don't have at least this spread, you won't have positive leverage if the loan is fully amortized. If you make interest-only payments, however, you will.

So, the general rule is that if you make interest-only payments, anytime your CAP rate is higher than your interest rate, you will have positive leverage. And, anytime you make fully-amortized payments and your CAP rate is at least 140 bps higher than your interest rate, you will have positive leverage. All other times, you have negative leverage.

In situations where you have positive leverage, it makes sense to try and obtain the largest loan possible, or put down as little money as the lender will allow. This is because as the leverage increases, so does your cash-on-cash return. If the LTV in example 1 were to increase from 75% to 85%, your cash-on-cash return would increase from 7.5% to 7.9%. And, if you were able to put only 5% down, or achieve a 95% LTV, your cash-on-cash return would balloon to 10.2%.

LTV	Cash-on-Cash Return
75%	7.5%
85%	7.9%
95%	10.2%

So, the idea is to get the best leverage you can and take advantage of a positive leverage situation. But, as we'll discuss below, you want to make sure that you've properly accounted for the cash flow so that if things don't go as planned, you don't end up on the wrong side of a highly-leveraged positive leverage deal.

Negative leverage, where your cash-on-cash return is lower than your CAP rate, means you're better off purchasing the property all cash (without debt). Now, this isn't necessarily true since it doesn't account for the effect of leverage, depreciation, appreciation, and tax shields. Interest expense is tax deductible; so even though you are in a negative leverage situation, you are gaining some tax shield from the mortgage payments you make.

The important point is that if the CAP rate is *lower* than the interest rate, your cash-on-cash return is *lower* than your CAP rate. In Example 2 above, if you were to purchase a 6.0% CAP property and finance it with debt at 6.5%, you'd only have a 1.1% return on a fully amortized loan. In these instances, lenders typically require larger down payments in order to meet the minimum DCR requirements. So in this example you'd most likely need to put 30%-35% down, rather than 25% down.

Through much of 2002-2006, investors found themselves in mostly positive-leverage situations. Interest rates were at all-time historic lows; and even though CAP rates were compressing and coming down, they still remained higher than the prevailing interest rates in the market. That all started to change in the fall of 2006; and by early 2007, many investors found themselves looking at negative-leverage deals. Interest rates had started to tick upward a little, and CAP rates had compressed to the point where it was difficult to find a deal with any positive leverage. This meant that most investors who made a decision to buy accepted the fact that their cash-on-cash returns were going to be somewhat meager at the outset of the investment. The only way to make any sense of most of those investments was for investors to convince lenders to offer them at least 1-3 years of I/O payments on the loan to offset the low initial CAP rate the property was being purchased at.

One of the main challenges with any investment is finding the right amount of leverage. Younger investors generally strive to put as little money down as possible, usually due to the fact they have such limited financial resources available to begin with. This usually limits them to SFRs, 2- to 4-unit buildings, and inexpensive multi-family investments. The problem, however, is that, oftentimes, younger investors and those in high LTV situations are under-capitalized and do not have the cash reserves available to weather any missteps in the investment.

To illustrate this point, I use one of my clients as a case study. This investor purchased multiple duplexes in a small town in Texas. There were 10 purchased in all, for a total of 20 units, all connected to one another. Since they were duplexes, the investor was able to get a residential loan with a 90% LTV. At the time of purchase, the rents for each unit averaged $1,000 a month and the local vacancy rate was approximately 6%. The setup on the properties at the time of purchase is shown below. Note that the Down Payment in this example includes closing costs equal to 2.5% of the purchase price. This figure totals $193,750, calculated as follows:

Down Payment = 10% * $1,550,000 = $155,000
Closing Costs = 2.5% * $1,550,000 = $38,750
Total Capital Invested = $155,000 + $38,750 = $193,750

Property Address:			Texas Dupluxes			
			Small Town, Texas			

Summary		Current Rents	Market Rents	Proposed Financing		
Price:		$1,550,000		**First Loan Amount:** $1,395,000	New	
Down Payment:	10%	$193,750		**Terms:** 5.75%	30 yr fixed	
Number of Units:		20				
Cost per Unit:		$77,500				
Current GRM:		6.46	6.46	*Brand new construction.		
Current CAP:		8.4%	8.4%	*10 duplexes.		
Year Built / Age:		2004		*$125/month PMI payment.		
Approx. Lot Size:		74,750				
Approx. Net RSF:		25,300				
Cost per Net RSF:		$61				

Annualized Operating Data

	Current Rents		Market Rents	
Scheduled Gross Income:	$240,000		$240,000	
Vacancy Rate Reserve[1]:	($14,400)	6.0%	($14,400)	6.0%
Gross Operating Income:	$225,600		$225,600	
Expenses:	($95,965)	-40.0%	($95,965)	-40%
Net Operating Income:	$129,635		$129,635	
Loan Payments:	($96,408)		($96,408)	
Pre-Tax Cash Flow[2]:	$33,227	17.1%	$33,227	17.1%
Principal Reduction:	$13,532		$13,532	
Total Return[2]:	$46,758	24.1%	$46,758	24.1%

[1] As a percent of Scheduled Gross Income

[2] As a percent of Down Payment.

Scheduled Income			CURRENT RENTS		MARKET RENTS		Estimated Expenses	
No. of Units	Bdrms/ Baths	Approx Sq. Ftg.	Monthly Rent/Unit ($)	Monthly Income ($)	Monthly Rent/Unit ($)	Monthly Income ($)	Taxes	$37,975
							Insurance	$18,140
							Utilities	$0
20	3+3	1,265	1,000	20,000	1,000	20,000	Gardener	$6,000
							Maint./Repairs	$9,600
							Off-Site Mgr.	$14,400
							Advertising	$250
							Misc/Reserves	$9,600
								$95,965
Total Scheduled Rent:			$20,000		$20,000			
Laundry:			$0		$0			
Other Income:			$0		$0			
Monthly Scheduled Gross Income:			$20,000		$20,000		Total Expenses:	$95,965
Annualized Scheduled Gross Income:			$240,000		$240,000		Per Net Sq. Ft.:	$3.79
Utilities Paid by Tenant:	All utilities						Per Unit:	$4,798.25

I've highlighted the important fields we're going to focus on. As you can see, each duplex was priced at $155,000, for a total cost of $1.55MM. The down payment required by the lender was 10%, or $155,000. The properties were operating at an 8.4% CAP at the time of purchase, and the projected cash-on-cash return was 17.1%. All in all, this represented a solid investment from a leverage- and cash-on-cash return standpoint. However, the total annual cash return only amounts to $33,227, or about $2,750 a month since the investor had only put $155,000 down ($193,750 with closing costs). So, the absolute return was not that substantial.

As time passed and my client began managing these properties, two things happened: Rents fell and the local vacancy rate increased. This was a direct result of overbuilding as the property was located in a smaller city with lots of inexpensive land available for development. By the end of Year 1, the property's setup had changed and looked as follows:

Property Address:		Texas Duplexes
		Small Town, Texas

Summary		Current Rents	Market Rents	Proposed Financing		
Price:		$1,550,000		First Loan Amount: $1,395,000		New
Down Payment:	10%	$193,750		Terms: 5.75%		30 yr fixed
Number of Units:		20				
Cost per Unit:		$77,500				
Current GRM:		7.18	6.46	*Brand new construction.		
Current CAP:		6.3%	8.6%	*10 duplexes.		
Year Built / Age:		2004		*$125/month PMI payment.		
Approx. Lot Size:		74,750				
Approx. Net RSF:		25,300				
Cost per Net RSF:		$61				

Annualized Operating Data

	Current Rents		Market Rents	
Scheduled Gross Income:	$216,000		$240,000	
Vacancy Rate Reserve[1]:	($25,920)	12.0%	($14,400)	6.0%
Gross Operating Income:	$190,080		$225,600	
Expenses:	($92,605)	-42.9%	($92,605)	-39%
Net Operating Income:	$97,475		$132,995	
Loan Payments:	($96,408)		($96,408)	
Pre-Tax Cash Flow[2]:	$1,067	0.6%	$36,587	18.9%
Principal Reduction:	$13,532		$13,532	
Total Return[2]:	$14,598	7.5%	$50,118	25.9%

[1] As a percent of Scheduled Gross Income
[2] As a percent of Down Payment.

Scheduled Income			CURRENT RENTS		MARKET RENTS		Estimated Expenses	
No. of Units	Bdrms/ Baths	Approx Sq. Ftg.	Monthly Rent/Unit ($)	Monthly Income ($)	Monthly Rent/Unit ($)	Monthly Income ($)	Taxes	$37,975
							Insurance	$18,140
							Utilities	$0
20	3+3	1,265	900	18,000	1,000	20,000	Gardener	$6,000
							Maint./Repairs	$8,640
							Off-Site Mgr.	$12,960
							Advertising	$250
							Misc/Reserves	$8,640
								$92,605
Total Scheduled Rent:			$18,000		$20,000			
Laundry:			$0		$0			
Other Income:			$0		$0			
Monthly Scheduled Gross Income:			$18,000		$20,000		Total Expenses:	$92,605
Annualized Scheduled Gross Income:			$216,000		$240,000		Per Net Sq. Ft.:	$3.66
Utilities Paid by Tenant:	All utilities						Per Unit:	$4,630.25

The local vacancy rate *doubled* from 6% to 12%, and rents fell from $1,000/month to $900/month. Neither economic indicator moved a terribly large amount, but the combination of the two was catastrophic. The investor's return dwindled to nothing and possibly a loss. While everyone believes this won't happen to them, the reality is that it happens more often than you realize. It's not unheard of for the vacancy in an area to increase from 6% to 12%. This can be the result of a number of things including newly developed residential units and/or rent concessions being given. As new developments are built and completed, the local housing stock supply increases; and this often drives rents down due to basic supply and demand. After all, if local population growth can't keep pace with local development, you have more supply than demand; and sale prices and rents *will* fall.

In this next example, if the investor had put 30% down instead of 10%, he would still have some positive cash flow ($34,157 per year) even if rents fell and vacancy rates increased. In this case, he would have tripled his down payment, or investment, and taken a much smaller loan. While he would have had to put more down to purchase the property, he would have had less chance of ending up in a cash-flow bind if the property's operations did not go as expected. And, since the investor put over 20% down, he is not required to make PMI (Personal Mortgage Insurance) payments of $1,250 per month, increasing his annual cash flow by $15,000. (Lenders require PMI when borrowers put down 20% or less. This helps protect them from the higher default rate among highly leveraged borrowers.)

It's reasonable to expect that if you purchase an investment where there's a good chance that a new development can and will be built in close proximity to yours, rents will fall and vacancies will rise unless there's enough unsatisfied demand to support the growth. We'll discuss this concept further, as well as the importance of doing a *Sensitivity Analysis* before you purchase an investment so that you fully grasp the impacts of new developments and other unforeseen risks. This example, however, clearly illustrates how being highly leveraged can turn from a positive into a negative.

Property Address:		Texas Dupluxes	
		Small Town, Texas	

Summary		Current Rents	Market Rents	Proposed Financing		
Price:		$1,550,000		First Loan Amount: $1,085,000		New
Down Payment:	30%	$503,750		Terms: 5.75%		30 yr fixed
Number of Units:		20				
Cost per Unit:		$77,500				
Current GRM:		7.18	6.46	*Brand new construction.		
Current CAP:		6.3%	8.6%	*10 duplexes.		
Year Built / Age:		2004		*No PMI payments - Buyer is putting at least 20% down.		
Approx. Lot Size:		74,750				
Approx. Net RSF:		25,300				
Cost per Net RSF:		$61				

Annualized Operating Data

	Current Rents		Market Rents	
Scheduled Gross Income:	$216,000		$240,000	
Vacancy Rate Reserve[1]:	($25,920)	12.0%	($14,400)	6.0%
Gross Operating Income:	$190,080		$225,600	
Expenses:	($92,605)	-42.9%	($92,605)	-39%
Net Operating Income:	$97,475		$132,995	
Loan Payments:	($63,318)		($63,318)	
Pre-Tax Cash Flow[2]:	$34,157	6.8%	$69,677	13.8%
Principal Reduction:	$10,525		$10,525	
Total Return[2]:	$44,682	8.9%	$80,202	15.9%

[1] As a percent of Scheduled Gross Income

[2] As a percent of Down Payment.

Scheduled Income			C U R R E N T R E N T S		M A R K E T R E N T S		Estimated Expenses	
No. of Units	Bdrms/ Baths	Approx Sq. Ftg.	Monthly Rent/Unit ($)	Monthly Income ($)	Monthly Rent/Unit ($)	Monthly Income ($)	Taxes	$37,975
							Insurance	$18,140
							Utilities	$0
20	3+3	1,265	900	18,000	1,000	20,000	Gardener	$6,000
							Maint./Repairs	$8,640
							Off-Site Mgr.	$12,960
							Advertising	$250
							Misc/Reserves	$8,640
								$92,605
Total Scheduled Rent:			$18,000		$20,000			
Laundry:			$0		$0			
Other Income:			$0		$0			
Monthly Scheduled Gross Income:			$18,000		$20,000		Total Expenses:	$92,605
Annualized Scheduled Gross Income:			$216,000		$240,000		Per Net Sq. Ft.:	$3.66
Utilities Paid by Tenant:	All utilities						Per Unit:	$4,630.25

Construction/A&D Loans. Construction loans, often called *Acquisition & Development* (A&D) *loans*, are used to purchase raw land or a property that is being redeveloped. These loans differ greatly from conventional loans and CMBS/LC loans and are primarily used for new construction, redevelopment, or condo conversions. In all instances, the property being purchased will most likely not generate income for many months or years from the time the purchase closes. This means that the operator or developer of the property will not have monthly income from the property to use to pay the debt service. As a result, the bank allows for an interest reserve in the loan amount so that the monthly interest due can be repaid at the time the whole loan is repaid, rather than on a monthly basis.

Here's an example of how it works. Some partners and I purchased a condo conversion project in Los Angeles in 2005. It was an existing 25-unit apartment building that had received Tentative Tract Map (TTM) approval from the City to convert the apartments to for-sale housing (condominiums). The TTM approval essentially allowed us to subdivide the property into 25 separate parcels that could then be resold on an individual basis as 25 condominiums. The process entailed our closing escrow on the purchase, then vacating all of the apartments so we could completely renovate them from apartment-quality to condo-quality. On a 25-unit building, this process could take 6 months or longer and cost $20,000 or more per unit.

In addition to money needed to buy the property, we also needed a loan to cover the remodeling expenses to improve the property to condo-quality. The cost of the property was $4.5MM, plus we had budgeted another $1.05MM for rehab and City permits and $.45MM for interest expense. The total project cost with financing was projected to be $6MM. The budget broke down as follows:

Purchase Price	$ 4,500,000
Rehab/Permits	$ 1,050,000
Interest Expense	$ 450,000
Total Project Cost	**$6,000,000**

The bank offered us an A&D loan which allowed us to purchase the property and begin the rehab work on the building. Part of the money loaned to us by the bank was called an "interest reserve." This is a set amount of money to be used to pay the debt service, or *carry cost*, on the loan while it's in use. In our case, we took a loan for a 12-month period. The total loan amount was $5MM at an interest rate of 9.0%. The bank required a down payment of the total project cost equal to 16.6%, which amounted to $1MM. The loan was to be extended for 12 months at 9.0%, which amounted to a total interest expense of $450,000, as calculated below:

Loan Amount	$ 5,000,000
Interest Rate	9%
Interest Expense	**$ 450,000**

The funds from an A&D loan are never distributed all at once, but rather in increments. The initial distribution is used to pay for the purchase, with the remaining funds dispersed over time in what is called a "construction draw." Typically, the bank requires receipts and possibly site visits after the current draw is spent and before they authorize the next draw. This is to make sure that monies aren't being squandered and that the project is moving along in a timely and proper fashion. Banks and lenders are not in the real estate business, and they do not want to find themselves taking a project back in the form of a foreclosure. The best way to avoid this is to dole the construction funds out in metered increments, making sure that the developer adheres to the project guidelines both parties agreed to.

In this example, after seven months of rehab work, the units were ready to be marketed to the public for sale. As a condition of the A&D loan, the bank allowed a "partial release" of the loan each time a unit was sold, since we started with one building and subdivided it into 25 separate units. As each unit sold, the provisions of the loan called for partial repayment and release of the loan. Each time we closed the sale of one of the condos, the proceeds from that sale were used to pay down the loan owed to the bank. The total retail value of the project was $7MM, leaving us $1MM in profit on our $1MM investment. Each unit sold for $280,000, and the proceeds from the first eighteen units sold went straight to the bank to repay the loan. The money from the remaining units was used to repay the initial Capital investment, plus a return on the investment.

An A&D loan is specifically designed to allow a developer to put off repayment of the loan until he begins to sell units and takes in cash. Once the project is ready for sale, repayment to the lender of principal and interest begins. A&D loans can be quite expensive to originate, with a total cost of 2%-3% of the loan amount. Leverage on these loans can range anywhere from 60% to as high as 97%. Typically, a lender places a 1st TD (First Trust Deed) on the project with a 75%-80% LTV, then a 2nd TD (Second Trust Deed) and, possibly, a 3rd TD (Third Trust Deed) may be placed, as well. The breakdown of debt might be as follows:

$$1^{st} \text{ TD } 75\%\text{-}80\% \text{ LTV}$$
$$2^{nd} \text{ TD } 5\%\text{-}15\% \text{ LTV}$$
$$3^{rd} \text{ TD } 3\%\text{-}5\% \text{ LTV}$$

As you move from the First Trust Deed to the Second Trust Deed to the Third Trust Deed, the cost of Capital, or interest rate, increases. This is because the 1st TD is in first position and is repaid first, making it the least risky of all debt lent on the property. The 2nd is repaid in the second position and the 3rd in the third. Therefore, the 3rd TD holder takes the greatest risk in the project. Many times, 2nd and 3rd TD debt is also called *mezzanine* debt (Mezz debt) or *equity*. The interest rate on the 1st TD is usually Prime + pricing such as 5.75% + 4.0%, for a total rate of 9.75%.

In this example, Prime would be the Index and 4.0% the margin. The rate on the 2nd TD can range from 2%-4% more than the 1st TD; and the interest on the 3rd can get to be very expensive, climbing as high as 27%-45% as happened in 2006, when Prime was in the low 5% range. That is why Mezz debt is also referred to as equity—because the interest rate is so high, the Mezz debt holder is often compensated with a similar return to the equity partners. The advantage of Mezz debt is that it allows developers to leverage up a project and have only 3%-5% equity in it. On a $100MM project, this totals no more than $3-5MM, and allows a developer to take on a very large project while putting up a small amount of at-risk Capital.

As you read this book, if you're considering a project that requires an A&D loan, I suggest you spend some time with your local lender to understand these loans better. Any project requiring an A&D loan is typically much more complicated than a standard income property investment, and has much higher risk associated with it. Make sure you understand the project you're considering and that you surround yourself with competent support people. These are the projects that can make and break careers; and one misstep can cause you to file bankruptcy.

PART IV: CASH-OUT REFIS –
WHEN DO THESE MAKE SENSE?

There will come a point in every real estate investment when you'll consider doing a cash-out refinance. A cash-out refinance is where you replace the existing loan with a new loan that's larger. When the new loan "funds," the proceeds are used to pay off the existing loan, and the remaining proceeds go to the borrower.

For example, on a 23-unit apartment building I owned in Los Angeles, the original purchase price was $3.5MM; and the original loan balance at the time of purchase was $2.5MM. After operating the property for 1 year and increasing the NOI by $60,000, I decided to do a cash-out refi. To do this, I contacted Washington Mutual (WAMU) and originated a new loan in the amount of $3.0MM. Once this loan funded, I used $2.5MM of the proceeds to pay off the original loan;

and the remaining $500K went into my savings account to be used for whatever purposes I chose, including future investments.

In order to do a cash-out refi, a few things need to happen. First, lenders usually like to see that you've owned the property for at least 12 months. This is called *seasoning*. There are some instances where they'll consider doing a refi sooner; but in general, 12 months is the minimum.

Second, the NOI on the property usually needs to have increased. After all, you're asking the lender for a larger loan than is currently on the property, and this translates into larger debt service payments. There's an exception, however, *if* rates have fallen. If the interest rate on your existing loan is 7.1%, and the rate on a new loan is 6.0%, you'll probably be able to do a cash-out refi and take out a larger loan even if your NOI has not increased. This is because your debt service payments will decrease since you're paying less interest expense each month due to the lower rate.

Lenders usually underwrite cash-out refis with different, more stringent guidelines than a new purchase. Typically, on new purchases, lenders are more aggressive and offer higher LTVs against lower DCRs. This translates into a larger loan amount. On cash-out refis, lenders usually will not go higher than a 75% LTV, and often no higher than 65%-70% LTV. So before you begin the process in earnest, you should check with a few lenders to find out what their guidelines are and whether they fit your needs.

Assuming the lender's guidelines do work for you, the next step is to provide the lender with all of the property-specific information including a current Rent Roll and Income/Expense Statement. Cash-out refis are just like regular loans in that they need to meet minimum DCR requirements. On refis, this number might be 1.25 vs. 1.15 on a new purchase. So, the most important factors in any cash-out refi are going to be the current NOI of the property and the prevailing interest rate.

You can't really affect the NOI of the property if you've currently maxed it out (meaning all your rents are at market); but you can affect the interest rate based on the program you choose. For example, a 10-year fixed loan might be priced at 6.875% while a 3-year fixed is at 6.125%. Typically, the 3-year fixed option gets you a larger loan amount since the annual debt service will be lower. It's a balance between the length of the fixed-rate term and your loan proceeds. You have to decide which is most important and arrive at a compromise between the two.

In the example above for my building in Los Angeles, I decided to go with a 7-year fixed. I would have preferred a 10-year fixed; but it would have resulted in a $90,000 smaller loan, and I really wanted access to the additional funds for another project.

Cash-out refis can be a great way to continue to move up the property ladder. The key to real estate is to make sure your equity is always working for you. Cash-out refis allow you to do this, as with my building in Los Angeles. By increasing the NOI by $60,000 during the first year of operating and ownership, I increased the value of the building. That gave me two choices: Sell and reinvest the proceeds and profit, or keep the building and do a cash-out refi and invest the proceeds. I chose the latter and used the refi proceeds as a down payment on another building in the same area. By repeating this pattern, over time you accumulate more property and larger buildings. Cash-out refis can be used in conjunction with 1031 Exchanges to help build your portfolio from one building to two buildings, to four buildings, and beyond. The key is to make sure that your equity is always working *for* you.

I always suggest to my clients that we sit down together and do an analysis of their portfolio every year. The goal is to evaluate how their properties are doing and identify underperforming assets. An underperforming asset is one that does not fully maximize its potential. That doesn't necessarily mean that it isn't doing well, just that it could be doing even better. One of our main goals is to identify properties that have increased NOIs or values. These are the properties that have the potential to create more investable equity through a cash-out refi.

By continually refinancing your properties and taking out more cash, you can continue to grow your portfolio without injecting new Capital. And since the bank requires you meet a minimum DCR, you're still going to generate annual cash flow. After all, the bank will NOT allow you to do a cash-out refi where you only break even. Remember, at a 1.25 DCR, you'll have positive-net (spendable) income every month. Over time, you'll not only increase your cash flow, but the size of your portfolio as well.

You'd benefit if you created a business plan for the next 5-10 years that maps out where you are today, where you'd like to end up, and the steps required to accomplish that goal. In my case, I began with a fourplex and now own a 23-unit apartment building. My goal is to purchase 40 more units over the next 5 years so I eventually own 60 units in total. Those 60 units should generate enough monthly income to support my lifestyle and allow me to do the things I want without being tethered to a 9-to-5 job.

CHAPTER 8 – RECONSTRUCTING THE OPERATING HISTORY: DOES THIS DEAL MAKE SENSE?

One of the most important things to understand in real estate is how to construct an *Operating History* and *Property Setup* for a potential investment. Many of your decisions will be based on the results you get from this exercise, and the setup you construct will serve as your point of reference throughout the decision-making process and ensuing purchase.

The Property Setup is how you'll be able to compare one investment opportunity to the next to make a decision on which one to purchase. I always use Microsoft Excel to do this, and I suggest you do the same. If you're not proficient in Excel, spend some time using the tutorial included with the software; and if you still want more practice, you can go online to find help or take a class at your local learning annex—or get someone you trust to assist you. I can't stress enough the value of being comfortable with this program and the Property Setup I'm about to walk you through. I've color-coded the Property Setup for this example, and included one on the CD Rom that was included with your purchase. The one that follows is not color coded, so make sure you are following along based on the Column and Row headings.

The first thing I always do when I find a property I might be interested in purchasing or evaluating for a client is to transfer all of the information on that property into my setup. The setup below is geared towards multi-family properties, but can also be used for retail and office space with very little variation.

Property Address:			123 Main Street USA Anytown, CA			

Summary		Current Rents	Market Rents	Proposed Financing		
Price:		$5,500,000		First Loan Amount:	$4,125,000	
Down Payment:	25%	$1,375,000		Terms:	6.450%	3 yr/30 yr am
Number of Units:		40				
Cost per Unit:		$137,500				
Current GRM:		9.82	9.21	*Excellent unit mix.		
Current CAP:		6.3%	7.0%	*Upside in rents.		
Year Built / Age:		1990				
Approx. Lot Size:		32,661				
Approx. Net RSF:		37,004				
Cost per Net RSF:		$149				

Property specific info - age, # units, lot size, $/SF, etc.

Proposed Financing - what type of loan can we get?

Operating Data - What does the income look like?

Scheduled Income - Unit mix, current income vs. market income

Estimated Expenses - how much does it cost to operate?

Annualized Operating Data					
	Current Rents			Market Rents	
Scheduled Gross Income:	$559,980			$597,180	
Vacancy Rate Reserve[1]:	($16,799)	3.0%		($17,915)	3.0%
Gross Operating Income:	$543,181			$579,265	
Estimated Expenses:	($196,294)	35.1%		($196,294)	32.9%
Net Operating Income:	$346,886			$382,970	
Loan Payments:	($311,248)			($311,248)	
Pre-Tax Cash Flow[2]:	$35,639	2.6%		$71,723	5.2%
Principal Reduction:	$41,250			$41,250	
Total Return[2]:	$76,889	5.6%		$112,973	8.2%

[1] As a percent of Scheduled Gross Income
[2] As a percent of Down Payment

Scheduled Income			CURRENT RENTS		MARKET RENTS		Estimated Expenses	
No. of Units	Bdrms/ Baths	Approx Sq. Ftg.	Monthly Rent/Unit ($)	Monthly Income ($)	Monthly Rent/Unit ($)	Monthly Income ($)	Taxes	$61,105
							Insurance	$13,000
							Utilities	$55,000
2	0+1	500-675	1,175	700	1,400		Gardener	$1,440
14	1+1	850-895	12,025	895	12,530		Rubbish	$3,750
3	2+1	1100-1200	3,415	1,250	3,750		Maint./Repairs	$17,500
13	2+2	1140-1295	15,575	1,295	16,835		On-Site Mgr.	$9,600
10	3+2	1350-1530	14,225	1,500	15,000		Off-Site Mgr.	$22,399
							Misc./Reserves	$12,500
Total Scheduled Rent:			$46,415		$49,515			$196,294
Laundry:			$250		$250			
Other Income:			$0		$0			
Monthly Scheduled Gross Income:			$46,665		$49,765		Total Expenses:	$196,294
Annualized Scheduled Gross Income:			$559,980		$597,180		Per Net Sq. Ft.:	$5.30
Utilities Paid by Tenant:		Electricity & Gas					Per Unit:	$4,907.36

Note: Current Rents monthly income values 1,175 / 12,025 / 3,415 / 15,575 / 14,225; Market Rents monthly Rent/Unit 700 / 895 / 1,250 / 1,295 / 1,500; Market Rents monthly income 1,400 / 12,530 / 3,750 / 16,835 / 15,000.

The above setup is divided into different sections. Each one has a purpose, and they all tie together to create the Cash-Flow Analysis worksheet we'll discuss after this. Below is a description of each section, what it tells you, and how to complete it using Excel.

Section 1: Property Address - The upper right-hand corner is where you enter the property's address.

Section 2: Property Information - Color-coded in light blue on the upper-left quadrant - This area is where you enter property-specific information as follows:

Price - How much is the asking price?

Down Payment - This figure is based on the loan quote you receive from your lender. The figure you want to change is the %; so

105

in this case, you could change the cell containing 25% to 30% or 35% based on the quote your lender comes back with. The cells are set to adjust automatically, so you don't need to change the down payment amount which is the cell just to the right of this one.

Number of Units - How many units does the property legally have?

Cost per Unit - This figure is automatically calculated by Excel once you enter the Purchase Price and Number of Units. This is a metric used by investors to compare similar investments. It's important to remember that this figure can be deceiving. For example, if one multi-family property has all 1-bedroom units and another has all 3-bedroom units, you'd expect the property with all 3-bedrooms units to have a higher Cost per Unit. Therefore, this figure can be useful in comparing one property to another; but, you need to understand the composition of the unit mix. After all, a 3-bedroom unit will always generate more monthly income than a 1-bedroom unit in a comparable property, so it will be worth more.

Current GRM/Current CAP - This also is automatically calculated by Excel once you enter the financial information into the other quadrants.

Year Built/Age - What year was the property built?

Approx. Lot Size - How many square feet is the lot the property sits on?

Approx. Net RSF - How many rentable square feet is the property? You can get this information from your agent or find it on the Title at the local Assessor's Office.

Cost per Net RSF - This is the $/RSF you're paying for the property and is automatically calculated by Excel. Many investors use this metric to compare similar investments. For instance, if you're looking to buy a multi-family property in Los Angeles with between 8-12 units and built after 1980, this is one way to compare available deals.

Section 3: **Proposed Financing** - Color-coded in bright green in the upper right-hand quadrant - This section deals with financing available for the property. In this area, the figures you enter are the **Interest Rate** and the **Term**. You get both from your lender based on the quote s/he provides to you. Excel automatically calculates the loan amount based on the Down Payment you enter in the Section above.

<u>Section 4</u>: **Operating Data** - This is the bright pink/purple section in the heart of the setup. The data in this area is calculated mostly by Excel, and there's very little for you to do here. In fact, the only figure you enter manually is the **Vacancy Rate Reserve**—and you don't enter the dollar amount, you enter the percentage. If the local vacancy rate is 10%, you change the 3% to 10% and Excel calculates the dollar amount. That's all you tinker with in this section.

<u>Section 5</u>: **Scheduled Income** - This is the light blue area on the bottom left of the worksheet and where you enter the rental/income data. It's the part of the spreadsheet where an investor goes to see what the unit mix of the property looks like, how much income it's generating today, and how much potential rental upside the property has. I consider this to be one of the most important parts of the worksheet since it details the property's income—and this is the reason you're purchasing it to begin with.

No. of Units - As you can see, this area is organized in a chart. For a multi-family property, you're going to have a number of different types of units ranging from bachelors/studios to 1-bedrooms, 2-bedrooms, and beyond. For an office/retail property, you might replace each unit type with a different office/retail space, numbering them by unit.

Bdrs/Bath - In this column, you enter the type of unit, i.e., a 1-bedroom/1-bath would be a 1+1. A 2-bedroom/1-bath would be a 2+1, and so on.

Approx. Sq. Ftg. - If you have the figure, enter the approximate (or exact) square footage of the unit. You can also leave this blank.

RENTS Monthly Rent/Unit ($) - In this column, you enter how much rent that unit type *currently* generates per month. Example: If you have five 1+1s, each renting for $450/month, enter $450 in this column. Sometimes, the property you're analyzing has multiple rents for the same unit *type*. There might be ten 1+1s in the building with rents ranging from $450-$485/month. In that case, you won't enter one figure, but rather the range as $450-485, as in the setup above.

RENTS Monthly Income ($) - Excel automatically calculates this column which shows how much total monthly rent is currently generated per unit type. Example: Your five 1+1s, each renting for $450/month, generate a total of $2,250/month in rent; so, this figure would be $2,250. However, if the property you're analyzing has multiple rents for the same unit type, you'll have to manually enter this figure. If the ten 1+1s from above generate a total of $4,650/month in income, enter this figure rather than have Excel calculate it.

MARKET RENTS Monthly Rent/Unit ($) - This next column is your estimate of the *potential* monthly rent that could be charged for that unit type. If your 1+1s currently rent for $450/month, but your neighbors charge $500/month, you might enter $500 in this column. This figure is based on the results of the rent survey you conducted in the area to ascertain what the local vacancy and market rents are; and, this is one of the most important figures in the worksheet, one you devote your time to determine. You want to make sure you estimate this figure as closely as possible without overestimating it. It's always better to be surprised than disappointed, so budget appropriately.

MARKET RENTS Monthly Income ($) — Excel automatically calculates this column which shows how much total monthly rent could potentially be generated if all units were at market rates. Example: You estimate that your five 1+1s could each rent for $500/month which would generate a total of $2,500/month in rent, so this figure would be $2,500.

Total Scheduled Rent - Excel automatically calculates this column which is the summation of all monthly rents per unit type and equals the total monthly rental income collected.

Laundry Income - Enter the monthly income currently generated by the laundry room in the first column (assuming there is an income-generating laundry facility at the property, which won't be the case for commercial/office property). This figure remains the same in the second column unless you feel you can increase it by adding more machines, increasing the cost to do a load of wash, or finding some other creative way to generate more monthly income. If you're using this worksheet for an office/retail project, you might change the name of this row to CAM (Common Area Maintenance) Charges, and enter the total monthly amount you'll receive from the tenants for CAM reimbursement.

Other Income - This might be income generated from additional parking, storage rental, or an Antenna Lease to a local cell phone carrier. Some properties do have additional income, others don't.

Monthly Scheduled Gross Income - Excel automatically calculates this column which is the total *monthly* income the property will generate.

Annualized Scheduled Gross Income - Excel automatically calculates this column which is the total *annual* income the property will generate.

Utilities Paid by Tenant - This lets you know which utilities the tenants pay for each month. Typically, you have water, electric, and gas, with all or part paid for by the landlord. Who pays for what varies by county and state. In Los Angeles, most properties are master-metered for water and sub-metered for gas and electric. This means the landlord pays the entire water bill and tenants pay their own gas and electric bills. The landlord will/may have an electric and gas bill for the laundry room and common area lighting. As a landlord, you'd like the tenant to pay for as many of the utilities as possible since you can't govern their use. For example, a 2+2 rented to a family of five will have a much higher water bill than a 1+1 rented to a single person. Tenants are more prone to conserve utilities and monitor their use when they're paying for the bill.

Section 6: Estimated Expenses - This is the bright yellow area on the bottom right of the worksheet. It's *very important* that you spend time making sure the figures you enter here are correct. Some of the expense information you receive will come from the Listing Agent on a deal, and you want to verify everything you're given and validate it with third-party sources.

Taxes - This cell usually contains a formula that Excel uses to calculate the annual tax figure. For example, in Los Angeles County, the average tax rate is 1.2%-1.25% of the purchase price. Enter the following formula into this cell:

=.012*Purchase Price

This formula recalculates the annual taxes on the property as you adjust the Purchase Price. The key to this cell is to *accurately* determine what the local tax rate is where you're buying, so it's important you talk to the local Tax Assessor's Office. Some cities reassess annually, others every two or three years. And some states, like California, don't reassess until a sale, but rather increase your payment by a maximum percentage as stipulated by law (it's 2% in CA). Property taxes vary by city and go from a low of around 1.2% in LA County to as high as 3.1% or more in some cities in Texas.

Taxes are one of your largest expenses, so it's imperative you make sure you use a correct figure. Don't be deceived by a Listing Package that shows what the current tax bill is. For many municipalities the figure will be recalculated once the property has sold and title is transferred; and, the new tax bill will be based on the sale price or a new reassessment.

Insurance - This figure should be based on an insurance quote you obtain during your Due Diligence period. Again, don't go with what the current owner pays for insurance. He may not have enough coverage, his deductible may be higher than you'd like, and the property premium may be bundled with other properties he owns. The most accurate figure will be based on a recent or current quote. You also want to speak with your lender to make sure they don't have any special requests regarding the policy.

Utilities - You get this figure from the current owner and verify it by going through 12-24 months of utility bills. This figure will most likely account for any gas, electric, and water bills for the property. You want to see a P&L (Profit & Loss Statement) for the past 2 years on the property and verify those figures against the utility bills you're provided. This will likely be your second largest expense after your tax bill. Again, you want to make sure you get this one right and that there aren't any hidden surprises.

Gardener - Ask the current owner for the past 12 months of invoices from his gardening or grounds maintenance crew. Contact the gardener and verify the amounts being charged and how much it will cost you to maintain his services once you take over ownership. If you feel this figure is high, get a few estimates from other local firms.

Rubbish - Also called trash collection. Ask the owner for a copy of 12 months of bills and call the service provider to verify they're correct. You might also ask them to make sure the current level of collection is sufficient to meet the property's needs. Some owners scale back their rubbish collection from 3x/week to 2x/week to save money, but it just ends up causing other issues for tenants. These are issues you don't want; so make sure you understand how many collections/week they recommend and what the cost will be. Again, if you feel the cost is high, contact other service providers for an estimate.

Maint/Repairs - This stands for Maintenance & Repairs. It's not free to keep a building properly maintained, and some months and years will be more expensive than others. The first thing you want to do is check the P&L you were given by the current owner to see how much money he's spent. You can then average this figure if you'd like to create a number moving forward. A word of caution: Many building owners fudge this figure; and, others don't maintain their properties in the condition you'd like or intend to. I always tell my clients to use a pro forma figure here rather than rely on what the current owner is spending. In LA County, lenders and property managers budget $400/unit/year for this line item. So, for a 20-unit building they might budget $8,000 a year to maintain the property. If you already own a building(s), you can see how much you currently spend and use that to estimate the cost of maintaining the property you're considering purchasing.

The key is to be realistic with this figure. Newer constructed properties will be less expensive to maintain than older properties. Copper plumbing will hold up better than galvanized plumbing, and sloped roofs will last longer than flat roofs. This is an area you don't want to underestimate since you want to make repairs as needed to maintain your property. After all, the better condition you keep it in, the better the tenant base you attract and the more it will be worth when you go to sell it.

On-site Mgr. - This is your on-site manager. Depending on the size of your property and local laws, you may or may not need an onsite manager. In LA County, all properties 16-units and larger must have an on-site manager. Check with the local Department of Housing to find out what the regulations are.

You also want to consider this decision from a practical standpoint. Retail/Office properties are generally managed by a combination of an on-site and off-site manager, and most of my clients employ a third-party management firm regardless of building size. Multi-family properties are usually managed with some combination of on-site and off-site management. Smaller multi-family properties with 9-units or less are often self-managed by the property investor(s).

It's usually reasonably easy for you to handle any leasing and maintenance issues as they arise with smaller properties. Once you get to 10-units and above, most investors find that using an on-site manager can be quite helpful. A good on-site manager will address most maintenance issues by either fixing them himself or calling a service provider to do so. He'll also handle any tenant issues and lease-up units as they become available. On-site managers are usually paid in the form of a rent subsidy or cash each month. My property manager for one of my buildings pays $595/month rent instead of the $1,295/month rent her unit is worth, effectively earning $700/month.

You should talk with your agent, other local investors, and management firms to ascertain what the appropriate amount is for this figure. It will vary by locale and the services you expect your manager to provide.

I always tell my clients who want to manage a property themselves to remember that their time is not free. Even if it only takes you 5 hours/week to manage the property, that's time you could spend elsewhere earning money. If your time is worth $40/hour (based on a 2,000 hour year at $80,000), those 5 hours/week are worth $200/week or $800/month. Make sure you pay yourself and account for your time accordingly.

Off-site Mgr. - The other half of the management equation is your off-site manager. Off-site management firms typically charge a percentage of the monthly GSI. As such, this cell is similar to the Taxes cell in that it's a formula that varies with the GSI of the property. You want to set this cell based on the percentage you expect to pay. If it's 5%, the formula would be as follows:

$$=.05 * \textbf{SGI Cell}$$

Management firms in LA County charge between 4%-6% of **SGI**. This amount varies by firm and the level of service they provide. Some handle basic management services like maintenance and leasing, while others also include bill paying and accounting. I suggest you contact 2-3 property management firms during your Due Diligence period to interview them and get an idea of what you can expect to pay.

As a side note, local property management firms can be a great way to find out more information about the property and area you're considering purchasing in. Many of these firms have been in business for years and there's even a chance they may have managed the property for a previous owner.

Misc/Reserves - Also known as Miscellaneous & Reserves and encompasses two things: First, any miscellaneous items not already accounted for such as annual Business License Registration, Pest Control, etc.; and second is Reserves, as in replacement reserves. For example, the roof on the property you're considering is probably a 15- to 20-year roof, which means that every 15-20 years it will need replacement—and that means you want/need to set aside a small amount of money every year in a Reserve Account so you have the cash available when a major Capital expenditure such as roof replacement comes along. If the estimated cost to replace the roof is $20,000, you want to set aside $1,000 per year in your Reserve Account. The same goes for other major items such as plumbing and electric upgrades. In LA County, many owners, lenders, and property managers use $400/unit/year for this figure. Speak with your agent and local property management firms to better estimate what the figure is in the area where you're buying.

Total Expenses - This figure is calculated by Excel and represents the total estimated annual expenses for the property you're analyzing.

Per Net Sq. Ft - This figure is calculated by Excel and represents the total estimated annual expenses per square foot for the property. This can be a useful figure when comparing properties and their expense loads. As mentioned, older buildings are typically more costly to operate than newer ones. Additionally, fully-amenitized properties with pools and elevators can also be more expensive due to the upkeep they require. One great, quick way to compare properties is the $/SF an owner will spend on expenses. This figure is especially relevant for retail/office space. An experienced investor can take a quick look at this figure and know right away whether the estimated expenses are realistic or not. In LA County, there's no way to operate an office building for less than $3.50/SF. So, if this investor were shown a property setup with a $3.00/SF expense ratio and an 8.5% CAP, the investor would know immediately that the CAP was probably inflated since the expenses were too low and need to be recalculated.

Per Unit - This figure is calculated by Excel and represents the total estimated annual expenses per unit for the property. It's the same metric as above, and just as useful, but more so with multi-family properties. Many experienced investors will tell you it's impossible to properly operate an apartment complex anywhere in the United States for less than $3,000/unit/year. If you see a setup or marketing package showing an 8.5% CAP and $1,800/unit/year in expenses, you know the CAP rate is incorrect. Again, this is a great metric to compare one property to another in the same local area. If one property operates at a considerably higher cost per unit than another, this is worth closer investigation. There may be an opportunity to create operational efficiencies and earn more money by doing some things better or more efficiently than the current owner does.

A final note on expenses: You're welcome to increase this section and add other line items if required. If the property has a pool and/or elevator, both items require expensive monthly service contracts that you want to itemize rather than group into a larger category; so, go ahead and make this list as detailed as possible. The purpose of this worksheet is to provide you with a comprehensive snapshot of how the property is operating today and what its future potential is.

Once you input all the data into this spreadsheet, you've created the Operating History and Setup of the property. This is the foundation of your Cash Flow statement and any other worksheets you want to create. Once you've done this a few times, it becomes quite easy for you. I suggest you practice by asking your agent for a few investment properties you can review. Create this worksheet for each to get more comfortable and familiar with each item. I've created thousands of these and can now fill one out in mere minutes; and the more you do it, the better you become at it.

CASH FLOW ANALYSIS

Now that you've constructed the Operating History and Setup, you're ready to create a Cash Flow worksheet. The Excel file I've provided is linked, so most of the work is done. Below is the second worksheet in that file titled, "5-Year Cash Flow Analysis." I'm going to walk you through each line so you can fully understand its meaning.

5 Year Cash Flow Analysis					
	Year 1	Year 2	Year 3	Year 4	Year 5
Scheduled Gross Income:	$597,180	$621,067	$645,910	$671,746	$698,616
Vacancy Rate Reserve:	($17,915)	($18,632)	($19,377)	($20,152)	($20,958)
Gross Operating Income:	$579,265	$602,435	$626,533	$651,594	$677,658
Estimated Expenses:	($196,294)	($202,183)	($208,249)	($214,496)	($220,931)
Net Operating Income:	$382,970	$400,252	$418,284	$437,098	$456,727
Loan Payments:	($311,248)	($311,248)	($311,248)	($311,248)	($311,248)
Pre-Tax Cash Flow:	$71,723	$89,004	$107,036	$125,850	$145,479
Cash on Cash Return	5.2%	6.5%	7.8%	9.2%	10.6%
Assumptions					
Annual Rent Increase	4.00%				
Annual Expense Increase	3.00%				

Scheduled Gross Income - Excel automatically calculates these figures. This was taken from the SGI figure on your Setup. In this example, I've assumed that rents increase annually by 4.00%, but you're free to change this figure as you please.

Vacancy Rate Reserve - Excel automatically calculates this figure, and it's based on the Vacancy percentage you entered on the Setup. This figure is subtracted from the SGI to arrive at the property's Gross Operating Income.

Gross Operating Income - Excel automatically calculates these figures. This is your GSI less your Vacancy Rate Reserve.

Estimated Expenses - Excel automatically calculates these figures. This was taken from the Estimated Expenses figure on your Setup. In this example, I've assumed that expenses increase annually by 3.00%, but you're free to change this figure as you please. Remember that if rents *are* increasing, we're in an *inflationary period* and expenses must be increasing as well.

Net Operating Income - Excel automatically calculates these figures, and they're a result of subtracting your Estimated Expenses from your Gross Operating Income.

Loan Payments - Excel will automatically calculate these figures, and they are based on the loan quote you received and the loan information you entered on the Setup.

Pre-Tax Cash Flow - Excel automatically calculates this figure, and it's arrived at by subtracting your Loan Payments from your NOI. This figure is expressed in dollars.

Cash-on-Cash Return - Excel automatically calculates this figure, and it's arrived at by dividing your Pre-Tax Cash Flow into your Down Payment (as shown in the upper-left of the Setup sheet). This figure should increase annually as your Pre-Tax Cash Flow increases, but your Down Payment remains the same. This figure is expressed as a percentage.

Now you've got your Property Setup and 5-Year Cash Flow Analysis worksheets done. You can change the hold period on the Cash Flow worksheet by shortening or lengthening the number of years you hold the property. Some investors want 3 years while others look at 7-10 years or more. The key is that you've got a worksheet where you can quickly review how the property is expected to perform. In this example you see that the investor's cash-on-cash return increases annually. This is due to the fact that his income increases by 4.0% each year, and his expenses by 3.0%. If you were to alter these figures, you'd get a different result. In the next chapter, we discuss *Sensitivity Analysis* and how you can use this information to forecast different scenarios and the likelihood of them occurring.

Chapter 9 - Discounted Cash Flow and Sensitivity Analysis: How Good is This Deal & Can I Make Money?

Now that we've constructed the Property Setup and Cash Flow worksheet, it's time to take the analysis a few steps further. The ultimate goal is to be able to calculate the IRR (Internal Rate of Return) of the project, as well as do a Sensitivity Analysis since this is one of the most important parts of underwriting an investment.

Let's assume you're considering purchasing a 19-unit property with an over 50% rental upside (as shown in the following setup). Since the building is not subject to rent control, you could begin raising rents shortly after you close escrow, and raise them as high as the market would bear. However, you should expect that some tenants will move when issued a very large rent increase (usually an increase of 15% or more).

In this example, you've got 1+1.5s renting for $625-$750/month when the prevailing rental rate in the local market is closer to $1,350 per month. So, it's reasonable to expect that some tenants will move when issued a 50% or more rent increase (taking them from $625/month to $1,350/month); and when they do, you need to plan on spending some money on light clean-up and rehab of the unit. This may include new flooring (carpet, tile, etc.), new fixtures in the kitchen and baths, new lighting, and fresh paint. In this example I've assumed the cost to be $3,000/unit, but you should confirm what your costs would be during your Due Diligence period.

If you plan to purchase a project that has good rental upside, it's a good idea to budget for rehab and clean-up expense because, depending on your plans for the property and the work required to update the units, this expense may be quite large. While this is not always the case, it's usually true that when you issue sizable rent increases to existing, long-term tenants who are paying well below market rents, a number of them will move. Depending on the level of rehab you plan on doing, you may actually be able to charge more than market rent since you'll be offering a premium rental unit.

Property Address:		123 Gordon Street
		Anytown, USA

Summary		Current Rents	Market Rents	Proposed Financing		
Price:		$2,300,000		First Loan Amount: $1,380,000	New	
Down Payment:	40%	$920,000		Terms: 6.000%	3 yr fix/30 yr am	
Number of Units:		19				
Cost per Unit:		$121,053				
Current GRM:		11.55	7.48	*Over 50% rental upside.		
Current CAP:		5.2%	9.8%			
Year Built / Age:		1985				
Approx. Lot Size:		13,098				
Approx. Net RSF:		13,468				
Cost per Net RSF:		$171				

Annualized Operating Data

	Current Rents		Market Rents	
Scheduled Gross Income:	$199,200		$307,620	
Vacancy Rate Reserve:	($5,976)	3.0%	-$9,229	3.0%
Gross Operating Income:	$193,224		$298,391	
Expenses:	($73,828)	-37.1%	-$73,828	-24%
Net Operating Income:	$119,396		$224,563	
Loan Payments:	($99,286)		-$99,286	
Pre-Tax Cash Flow:	$20,110	2.2%	$125,277	13.6%
Principal Reduction :	13,800		13,800	
Total Return:	$33,910	3.7%	$139,077	15.1%

[1] As a percent of Scheduled Gross Income
[2] As a percent of Down Payment.

Scheduled Income			RENTS		MARKET RENTS		Estimated Expenses [3]	
No. of Units	Bdrms/ Baths	Approx Sq. Ftg.	Monthly Rent/Unit ($)	Monthly Income ($)	Monthly Rent/Unit ($)	Monthly Income ($)	Taxes	$25,530
							Insurance	$6,175
							Utilities	$12,686
1	0+1		500	700	895	895	Gardener	$1,200
16	1+1.5	TH	625-750	14,000	1,350	21,600	Rubbish	$1,778
2	2+1.5	TH	800-850	1,750	1,495	2,990	On-Site Mgr.	$6,000
							Off-Site Mgr.	$9,960
							Maint./Repairs	$5,500
							Misc/Reserves	$5,000
								$73,828
Total Scheduled Rent:			$16,450		$25,485			
Laundry:			$150		$150			
Other Income:			$0		$0			
Monthly Scheduled Gross Income:			$16,600		$25,635		Total Expenses:	($73,828)
Annualized Scheduled Gross Income:			$199,200		$307,620		Per Net Sq. Ft.:	($5.48)
Utilities Paid by Tenant:	Electric & Gas						Per Unit:	($3,885.71)

For example, in one of my buildings (23 units in LA County), I replaced all the laminate kitchen counters with granite, installed all new lighting and Pergo (laminate hardwood) flooring, and painted the units in two-tone colors. By doing this, I was able to charge $200 more a month than my neighbors charged for a comparable 1+1. I spent

$9,000 per unit on rehab and clean-up, and was able to raise the rent by $2,400/year (or $200/month), My payback period was 45 months calculated as follows:

Payback Period = $9,000 spent on rehab/$200 per month additional rent = 45 months

My return on investment (ROI) for the rehab funds spent on that unit was 26.7%, calculated as follows:

ROI = $2,400 per year additional rent/$9,000 spent on rehab = 26.7%

As you can see, it made sense for me to spend the additional money on rehab since my additional investment was returning over 26% annually. By increasing the monthly rent per unit, I increased the overall GSI of the property which, in turn, increased the building's total value. The GSI on my 23-unit building increased by $60,000 per year, which based on a 6.0% CAP, equated to an additional $1MM in value, calculated as follows:

Additional Value = $60,000 per year GSI/6.0% CAP = $1,000,000

The point is that you want to make sure you carefully plan and budget all rehab work and understand how much you're going to spend and how long it will take to recoup those monies. I spent $180,000 total ($9,000 per unit for 20 units) and increased my annual income by $60,000, earning a 33% return on my additional investment, increasing my property's value by $1MM. Rehabbing your investment and making sure you earn top-dollar rents can have an immediate impact on your bottom line, as well as an even larger impact when you go to sell, refinance, or do a 1031 Exchange.

IRR

IRR (Internal Rate of Return) is a somewhat complicated mathematical concept. In laymen's terms, the IRR is the average annual return which is earned on your invested Capital, and is also known as the *yield* on the investment. I usually equate this to a client's mutual fund portfolio. Most funds report their 1-, 5-, and 10-year annualized rates of return in their annual reports. These figures closely resemble the IRR of a mutual fund, which is why this is probably the simplest way to think about the IRR of an investment.

An investment is considered worthwhile if its IRR is greater than the rate of return you could earn investing the funds elsewhere (i.e., stocks, bonds, mutual funds, etc.). If the IRR of a multi-family project is projected to be 12.6% and the total investment is $1MM, it would be a solid investment if your alternative was to take those funds and put them in an S&P 500 mutual fund earning 10.8% annually.

It's important to note that IRRs are *not* risk-adjusted and do not account for the underlying risk of a project or investment. So, you can't compare a CD on deposit with your bank earning 5% to a ground-up construction project with a 5% IRR. The CD is one of the safest investments you can make while the ground-up construction project is quite risky. If you're going to take on the additional risk inherent with the latter investment, you should be rewarded with a comparable *bump* to your IRR. It's difficult to quantify what the figure should be since everyone has a different appetite for risk; but most investors would agree that if your alternatives were a 5% CD or the ground-up project, the latter should provide the potential for at least a 12%-15% IRR over the same hold period.

In general, most investors will consider a project or investment if the IRR is greater than their *hurdle rate*. An investor's hurdle rate is the *minimum* rate of return he wants to earn on the Capital he has available to invest. For example, one of my clients likes to earn at least 10% on his money, so I won't show him any deals that don't have at least a 10% IRR. Every investor's hurdle rate is different; and your hurdle rate usually declines as you get older, have accumulated more wealth and Capital, and become more risk-averse.

Returning to the 19-unit multi-family example, I've included a copy of the Cash Flow Analysis below. This time, notice that I've also added an IRR and NPV (Net Present Value) calculation. The NPV of an investment is how much money an investor would earn above his hurdle rate. In this example we assume the investor has a hurdle rate of 6%. If the investor were to use his funds to purchase this 19-unit building rather than invest them in a 6% CD, he would earn an additional $1,780,175 over the 7-year investment period. As you increase your hurdle rate the NPV will fall, eventually going to $0. The point where this occurs is where your hurdle rate is equal to the IRR of the project. In this example if your hurdle rate was 26.7%, your NPV would be $0. Basically, you'd gain nothing by purchasing this 19-unit building versus investing your funds in a CD paying 26.7% annually since both would yield the same total return over a 7-year period.

Cash Flow Analysis								
	Year 1	Year 2	Year 3	Year 4	Year 5	Year 6	Year 7	
Scheduled Gross Income:	$199,200	$307,620	$319,925	$332,722	$346,031	$359,872	$374,267	
Vacancy Rate Reserve:	($5,976)	($9,229)	($9,598)	($9,982)	($10,381)	($10,796)	($11,228)	
Gross Operating Income:	$193,224	$298,391	$310,327	$322,740	$335,650	$349,076	$363,039	
Estimated Expenses:	($73,828)	($74,936)	($76,060)	($77,201)	($78,359)	($79,534)	($80,727)	
Less CAP EX	($36,000)	$0	$0	$0	$0	$0	$0	
Net Operating Income:	$83,396	$223,456	$234,267	$245,539	$257,291	$269,542	$282,312	
Loan 1st TD	($99,286)	($99,286)	(99,286)	(99,286)	(99,286)	(99,286)	(99,286)	
Pre-Tax Cash Flow:	($15,890)	$124,170	$134,982	$146,254	$158,005	$170,256	$183,026	
Cash on Cash Return	-1.7%	13.5%	14.7%	15.9%	17.2%	18.5%	19.9%	
Property Value	1,389,926	3,724,259	3,904,453	4,092,322	4,288,182	4,492,359	4,705,193	
Property Value in Year 7	4,705,193							
Less Disposition Costs	(258,786)							
Cash at Sale in Year 7	4,446,407							
Gain Upon Sale	3,191,407							
Cash Flow Stream	(920,000)	(15,890)	124,170	134,982	146,254	158,005	170,256	3,374,433
IRR	26.7%							
NPV Discount Rate	6.0%							
NPV	1,780,175							
Rent Increase Assumption	4.00%							
Disposition Cap Rate	6.00%							
Disposition Costs	5.50%							
Principal Reduction	125,000							

Notice that I've also added an additional row to our Cash Flow Analysis titled LESS CAP EX, taking into account the Capital Expenditures (CAP EX) for rehab and clean-up. It totals $36,000 for Year 1, and is based on spending $3,000/unit on 12 units, total. I'm showing this expense only in Year 1 since my "plan" is to raise all rents to market rate immediately upon close of escrow, and plan to have the property fully stabilized by the end of Year 1. If your project were larger or your timeline longer, you might have additional CAP EX expenses in Year 2 and beyond; or, you may decide to postpone doing any CAP EX work until Year 2, in which case you would have no CAP EX expenses in Year 1. The point is to properly account for this additional expense which would *not* fall under your normal Operating Expenses.

I've also added a Property Value row. This figure is automatically calculated by Excel and is the product of dividing the current year's NOI by the *Disposition CAP Rate* (explained in the next paragraph). For example, in Year 2 you'd have the following:

Property Value = $223,456/.06 = $3,724,259

The Disposition CAP Rate is a figure you have to estimate since it requires you to predict what the prevailing CAP Rate will be in the marketplace seven years from now. Since you don't have a crystal ball, this is going to be a guesstimate on your part. I always suggest to investors/clients to use caution here and be conservative. If you think values are going to rise in the future, you forecast a lower CAP Rate than the one you purchased the property for.

If you bought a property at a 6.0% CAP and thought that values were going to increase and that CAP Rates were going to compress (get smaller), you'd forecast a Disposition CAP Rate of 5.5% or lower. Since a property's value is directly tied to its NOI and CAP Rate, if the NOI remains constant or flat, meaning no rental income growth, the only way the property value can increase is by CAP Rates declining. So, if CAP Rates were to fall from 6.0% at time of Purchase to 5.0% at time of Sale, values would increase by 20%, calculated as follows:

	Sale	Purchase
NOI	$ 1,000,000	$ 1,000,000
Cap	5.00%	6.00%
Value	$ 20,000,000	$ 16,666,667
% Increase	20.0%	

In this example, I'm assuming you have a property generating an NOI of $1MM. You purchase it at a 6.0% CAP Rate, which values it at $16.67MM. When you go to sell it some time in the future, your NOI has remained the same (no rental growth) at $1MM. During your hold period, CAP Rates have compressed, or fallen, and values have increased, and someone is willing to purchase your property at a 5.0% CAP Rate, or $20MM. You have just realized a 20% increase in value without any rental growth.

It's very important to understand that the value of a property *increases* when the CAP Rate in the market place falls, and the NOI remains constant. Using our property with a $1MM NOI, I've created the following table and chart to illustrate this point.

CAP Rate	Property Value
4.00%	$25,000,000
4.50%	$22,222,222
5.00%	$20,000,000
5.50%	$18,181,818
6.00%	$16,666,667
6.50%	$15,384,615
7.00%	$14,285,714
7.50%	$13,333,333
8.00%	$12,500,000
8.50%	$11,764,706
9.00%	$11,111,111
9.50%	$10,526,316
10.00%	$10,000,000

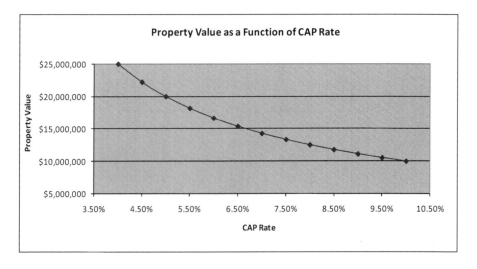

As the CAP Rate increases from 4.0% to 10.0%, the property's value decreases from $25MM to $10MM, all at the same NOI of $1MM. This is very powerful information since the value of your property can increase due to market forces, alone, and *without* income (NOI) growth.

Returning to guessing what CAP Rates will be sometime in the future; the key is to make sure you're realistic and conservative. It's better to be surprised than disappointed. You want to make sure you understand *where* you're buying relative to historical values and what the economic outlook is for the future. For example, the historical CAP

Rates that multi-family properties have traded at is between 7.5-8.0%. In 2006 in LA County, multi-family CAP Rates were in the 5.75%-6.0% range, which was close to their historical lows. Anyone buying in 2006 could reasonably assume that CAP Rates would either remain flat or increase over time, but not likely compress further since they were already at historical lows.

Since I don't have a crystal ball, I advise most clients to assume that their Disposition CAP Rate will be equal to or higher (usually .5%-1.0%) than their purchase CAP Rate. If you purchase a property at a 6.0% CAP, you might assume a 6.5%-7.0% Disposition CAP Rate. As you'll see below, overestimating this figure can have a huge effect on your IRR and over-inflate it. In fact, if you play around with the spreadsheet, you'll see that every additional .5% CAP can make a very large difference to your IRR.

In order to calculate the IRR of any project, you need to create a schedule of cash flows. On the spreadsheet, this is the row labeled *Cash Flow Stream*. In Year 1 (the first column), we have a large negative figure ($920,000), which is your down payment and closing costs to purchase the property. In the next cell, you input any cash flow/loss generated from operations in Year 1. In this case, the property had a Pre-Tax Cash Flow of -$15,890 (a loss), so that is the figure you would enter. Remember, since you're turning over 12 units, or more than 60% of the property, you're going to lose money due to rehab costs. However, it's possible that in Year 1 you could operate at a profit if your rehab costs were not too great (i.e., you turned over fewer units than you anticipated).

Into the next cell goes the cash flow/loss generated from Year 2, and so on and so forth, until you reach the end of the project. In this example, we're using a 7-year hold period, so there will be eight cells, total, comprising the Cash Flow Stream row. The cash flow/loss in the final cell is comprised of the annual cash flow from operations for Year 7, as well as the proceeds from the sale of the property in Year 7. After all, when you go to the sell the property you'll have realized a gain or a loss. To calculate this value you do the following:

Gain Upon Sale = Property Value at Time of Sale - Disposition Costs - Original Loan Amount + Principal Reduction
Gain Upon Sale = $4,705,193 - $258,786 - $1,380,000 + $125,000

The first value, $4,705,193, was calculated by dividing the Year 7 NOI by the Disposition CAP Rate. The $258,786 figure is the cost of sale, which represents 5.5% of the $4,705,193 Property Value at time of sale. The 5.5% figure will vary by locale, but is comprised of title/escrow fees, broker fees, all applicable transfer taxes, and any other costs associated with the sale. Remember, it's not free to sell real estate.

The $1,380,000 is the original loan amount on the property. The $125,000 is the amount of principal reduction paid over the hold period. This figure can be calculated by creating an amortization table in Excel, or more easily by visiting a website that has a mortgage calculator (which is my preferred method).

Note that if you had an interest-only mortgage, you would not have paid down any principal over the hold period and would owe the bank the original loan amount. Also, if you refinanced the loan during the hold period, you'd have paid off the original 1st Trust Deed (TD—your mortgage) and replaced it with another loan at a different amount. In the case of a cash-out refinance, you would have replaced the original loan with a larger loan. At that time, you would also have received "cash out" and those monies should be figured into your IRR.

I've changed our example to assume a cash-out refi in Year 4, as shown below.

Cash Flow Analysis							
	Year 1	Year 2	Year 3	Year 4	Year 5	Year 6	Year 7
Scheduled Gross Income:	$199,200	$307,620	$319,925	$332,722	$346,031	$359,872	$374,267
Vacancy Rate Reserve:	($5,976)	($9,229)	($9,598)	($9,982)	($10,381)	($10,796)	($11,228)
Gross Operating Income:	$193,224	$298,391	$310,327	$322,740	$335,650	$349,076	$363,039
Estimated Expenses:	($73,828)	($74,936)	($76,060)	($77,201)	($78,359)	($79,534)	($80,727)
Less CAP EX	($36,000)	$0	$0	$0	$0	$0	$0
Net Operating Income:	$83,396	$223,456	$234,267	$245,539	$257,291	$269,542	$282,312
Loan 1st TD	($99,286)	($99,286)	(99,286)	(99,286)	(204,616)	(204,616)	(204,616)
Pre-Tax Cash Flow:	($15,890)	$124,170	$134,982	$146,254	$52,675	$64,925	$77,695
Cash on Cash Return	-1.7%	13.5%	14.7%	15.9%	-14.2%	-17.5%	-20.9%
Property Value	1,389,926	3,724,259	3,904,453	4,092,322	4,288,182	4,492,359	4,705,193
Property Value in Year 7	4,705,193						
Less Disposition Costs	(258,786)						
Cash at Sale in Year 7	4,446,407						
Gain Upon Sale	1,824,392						
Cash Flow Stream	(920,000)	(15,890)	124,170	134,982	1,438,269	52,675	64,925	1,902,087
IRR	31.1%						
NPV Discount Rate	6.0%						
NPV (Net Present Value)	1,677,571						
Assumptions							
Rent Increase Assumption	4.00%						
Disposition Cap Rate	6.00%						
Disposition Costs	5.50%						
Principal Reduction	50,000						
Assume a Cash Out Refi in Year 4							
Expected NOI	$245,539						
Expected DCR	1.20						
Expected Interest Rate	6.50%						
Maximum Debt Service	$ 204,616						
Maximum Loan Amount	$ 2,672,016						
Equity In Deal	$ (372,016)						
Equity Returned	$1,292,016						

NOI, and has nothing to do with how you finance the property. What *does* change is your Cash Flow Stream and Debt Service Payment. Assume that you do the cash-out refi at the end of Year 4, with the funds coming right at Dec. 31. Since you've increased the NOI on the property from $83,396 in Year 1 to $245,539 in Year 4, the property is able to debt service a much larger loan. In this case, your NOI increased by 194%, calculated as follows:

NOI Increase = 194% = ($245,539 - $83,396)/$83,396

Your loan amount has increased from $1,380,000 to $2,672,016, based on a 1.20 DCR. With the higher loan comes a larger mortgage payment each year, going from $99,286 to $204,616. The positive effect of the cash-out refi is that you now have an additional $1,292,016 you can invest wherever you'd like. This also increases your Cash Flow Stream by the same amount in that year. Notice that your Cash Flow jumps to $1,438,269 that year, with the majority of it coming from the refi proceeds.

By doing a cash-out refi, you increase the IRR of the investment from 26.7% to 31.1% over the hold period. Also, your cash-on-cash returns, after the refi, increase dramatically. In this example, the total cash you're able to take out from the refi is greater than your original investment ($1,292,016 is greater than $920,000). This means that your original $920,000 investment is returned, plus you receive additional funds as well. At this point, you no longer have any equity in the deal. This is why the Cash-on-Cash figures in Year 5 and beyond are negative: You're earning a return on a deal that you have no equity in. This situation doesn't happen often; but if you find the right property with a lot of upside, it can occur.

This will not always be the case; and many times, the increased NOI at the time of the refi will only be large enough to allow you to take out some of your original equity, with the remainder of it still in the deal. In that instance, your Cash-on-Cash return will be calculated based on the new amount of equity in the deal, not the original amount. So, if in this example the cash-out refi only provided you with $500,000 rather than $1,292,016, you'd still have $420,000 left in the deal ($920,000 less $500,000). In that case, your Cash-on-Cash in Year 5 and beyond would be calculated against $420,000 in equity, rather than your original $920,000. So, in Year 5 your Cash-on-Cash would be calculated as follows:

$52,675/$420,000 = 12.5%

I know that the above process seems somewhat complicated; however, it's very important you read through it as often as it takes to fully understand the concepts. Most of the figures are automatically calculated by Excel, with the exception being your *assumptions*. Once you complete the Property Setup, all the figures flow from this worksheet onto the next worksheet and your Cash Flow Analysis is complete. All that's left is for you to change the NPV Discount Rate, Rent Increase Assumption, Disposition CAP Rate, and Disposition Costs cells. Don't get mired in the math; rather, focus on the broad concepts. Understand that increasing your NOI each year increases the property's value, and that assuming a lower Disposition CAP Rate also increases the property's value and the project's IRR.

SENSITIVITY ANALYSIS

Once you've created your Property Setup and Cash Flow worksheets and computed the IRR of your potential investment, the next step is to do a Sensitivity Analysis. This helps you find out how much room for error there is in your assumptions, and if the project is feasible if unexpected conditions were to occur. Part of your Sensitivity Analysis is to perform a *break-even analysis* to find out how high local vacancies can rise and how far rents can fall before you're no longer able to make your monthly debt service payments.

Going back to the duplex example in Texas, let me show you how to perform a break-even analysis.

Following is the setup for the expected scenario where units rent for $1,050 per month and the local vacancy rate holds steady at 6.0%. What happens, however, if one or both of these assumptions proves incorrect? After all, what could go wrong with our projections? First, your rental projections could be incorrect, or rental rates could fall. Second, the vacancy rate in the area could increase; and third, our expense projections could be off.

Property Address:	Texas Dupluxes
	Small Town, Texas

Summary	Current Rents	Market Rents	Proposed Financing	
Price:	$1,550,000		First Loan Amount: $1,395,000	New
Down Payment: **10%**	$193,750		Terms: 5.75%	30 yr fixed
Number of Units:	20			
Cost per Unit:	$77,500			
Current GRM:	6.15	6.15	*Brand new construction.	
Current CAP:	9.0%	9.0%	*10 duplexes.	
Year Built / Age:	2004		*$125/month PMI payment.	
Approx. Lot Size:	74,750			
Approx. Net RSF:	25,300			
Cost per Net RSF:	$61			

Annualized Operating Data

	Current Rents		Market Rents	
Scheduled Gross Income:	$252,000		$252,000	
Vacancy Rate Reserve[1]:	($15,120)	**6.0%**	($15,120)	6.0%
Gross Operating Income:	$236,880		$236,880	
Expenses:	($97,645)	-38.7%	($97,645)	-39%
Net Operating Income:	$139,235		$139,235	
Loan Payments:	($96,408)		($96,408)	
Pre-Tax Cash Flow[2]:	$42,827	22.1%	$42,827	22.1%
Principal Reduction:	$13,532		$13,532	
Total Return[2]:	$56,358	29.1%	$56,358	29.1%

[1] As a percent of Scheduled Gross Income
[2] As a percent of Down Payment.

Scheduled Income			CURRENT RENTS		MARKET RENTS		Estimated Expenses	
No. of Units	Bdrms/ Baths	Approx Sq. Ftg.	Monthly Rent/Unit ($)	Monthly Income ($)	Monthly Rent/Unit ($)	Monthly Income ($)	Taxes	$37,975
							Insurance	$18,140
							Utilities	$0
20	3+3	1,265	1,050	21,000	1,050	21,000	Gardener	$6,000
							Maint./Repairs	$10,080
							Off-Site Mgr.	$15,120
							Advertising	$250
							Misc/Reserves	$10,080
								$97,645
Total Scheduled Rent:			$21,000		$21,000			
Laundry:			$0		$0			
Other Income:			$0		$0			
Monthly Scheduled Gross Income:			$21,000		$21,000		Total Expenses:	$97,645
Annualized Scheduled Gross Income:			$252,000		$252,000		Per Net Sq. Ft.:	$3.86
Utilities Paid by Tenant:	All utilities						Per Unit:	$4,882.25

What if our rental projections are off, and how could this happen? If you do a good rent survey and analyze multiple properties in the local area, you should end up within +/- 3%-5% of the actual rents you'll be able to realize. Additionally, the income the building currently generates is usually a good starting point, unless the Seller has manipulated the leases by offering tenants move-in concessions that you're unaware of at the time of purchase. For example, let's assume the Seller offered each tenant the first month rent-free, effectively creating an 8.3% economic vacancy, calculated as follows:

Economic Vacancy = 1 month Free Rent/12-month Lease = 8.3%

As you can see, if you offer a tenant 1 rent-free month on a 12-month lease, you effectively have an 8.3% economic vacancy rate. This is one way your rents could be off. The second, and more likely scenario, is that an overall shift occurs in the local or national economy causing rents to fall. Rental rates are governed by *Supply & Demand*, so if rents fall, it's usually due to an increase in supply or a decrease in demand.

An increase in supply might be due to the completion of new housing units in the local area while a decrease in demand might occur due to the loss of a local employment base. If some new developments were built within 1-2 miles of your property, the total available rental inventory would increase, driving down rental rates until the new units were absorbed, or rented. In some areas, like LA County, this isn't generally a problem since demand for housing far outstrips supply. In fact, it's estimated there is a 200,000-unit housing shortage in LA County, with only a few thousand new units coming available each year.

The second possibility, a loss of a local employment base, occurred in LA County in the early 1990s with the exodus of the aerospace industry to other markets. This took away many well-paying jobs and helped throw the area into a recession. All of sudden, you had many mid-level managers and engineers with no job prospects who were unable to make their monthly rent payments. They were forced to seek employment elsewhere, thereby reducing the demand for housing. When this occurs, rental rates fall, as they did.

Going back to the example above, we want to find out how far rental rates can fall and how high vacancy rates can rise before we have trouble making our mortgage payment. We want to isolate each metric, thereby solving for two separate answers. First, we'll find out how far rents can fall. To do this, simply keep lowering the rental rate of $1,050 per month until your cash-on-cash return falls to $0. As you see below, the answer is $828. So, if rents were to fall from $1050/month to $828/month, you would break even every month, but would not earn a profit.

Property Address:	Texas Dupluxes
	Small Town, Texas

Summary	Current Rents	Market Rents	Proposed Financing	
Price:	$1,550,000		First Loan Amount: $1,395,000	New
Down Payment: 10%	$193,750		Terms: 5.75%	30 yr fixed
Number of Units:	20			
Cost per Unit:	$77,500			
Current GRM:	7.80	6.15	*Brand new construction.	
Current CAP:	6.2%	9.5%	*10 duplexes.	
Year Built / Age:	2004		*$125/month PMI payment.	
Approx. Lot Size:	74,750			
Approx. Net RSF:	25,300			
Cost per Net RSF:	$61			

Annualized Operating Data

	Current Rents		Market Rents	
Scheduled Gross Income:	$198,720		$252,000	
Vacancy Rate Reserve[1]:	($11,923)	6.0%	($15,120)	6.0%
Gross Operating Income:	$186,797		$236,880	
Expenses:	($90,186)	-45.4%	($90,186)	-36%
Net Operating Income:	$96,611		$146,694	
Loan Payments:	($96,408)		($96,408)	
Pre-Tax Cash Flow[2]:	$203	0.1%	$50,286	26.0%
Principal Reduction:	$13,532		$13,532	
Total Return[2]:	$13,734	7.1%	$63,817	32.9%

[1] As a percent of Scheduled Gross Income

[2] As a percent of Down Payment.

Scheduled Income			CURRENT RENTS		MARKET RENTS		Estimated Expenses	
No. of Units	Bdrms/ Baths	Approx Sq. Ftg.	Monthly Rent/Unit ($)	Monthly Income ($)	Monthly Rent/Unit ($)	Monthly Income ($)	Taxes	$37,975
							Insurance	$18,140
							Utilities	$0
20	3+3	1,265	828	16,560	1,050	21,000	Gardener	$6,000
							Maint./Repairs	$7,949
							Off-Site Mgr.	$11,923
							Advertising	$250
							Misc/Reserves	$7,949
								$90,186
Total Scheduled Rent:				$16,560		$21,000		
Laundry:				$0		$0		
Other Income:				$0		$0		
Monthly Scheduled Gross Income:				$16,560		$21,000	Total Expenses:	$90,186
Annualized Scheduled Gross Income:				$198,720		$252,000	Per Net Sq. Ft.:	$3.56
Utilities Paid by Tenant: All utilities							Per Unit:	$4,509.29

We can perform a similar calculation for the Vacancy Rate, and find that local vacancies can rise to 22.9% and still allow you to break even each month while paying all your expenses and mortgage.

131

Property Address:				Texas Duplexes			
				Small Town, Texas			

Summary		Current Rents	Market Rents	Proposed Financing			
Price:		$1,550,000		First Loan Amount: $1,395,000		New	
Down Payment:	10%	$193,750		Terms: 5.75%		30 yr fixed	
Number of Units:		20					
Cost per Unit:		$77,500					
Current GRM:		6.15	6.15	*Brand new construction.			
Current CAP:		6.2%	9.0%	*10 duplexes.			
Year Built / Age:		2004		*$125/month PMI payment.			
Approx. Lot Size:		74,750					
Approx. Net RSF:		25,300					
Cost per Net RSF:		$61					

Annualized Operating Data

	Current Rents		Market Rents	
Scheduled Gross Income:	$252,000		$252,000	
Vacancy Rate Reserve[1]:	($57,708)	22.9%	($15,120)	6.0%
Gross Operating Income:	$194,292		$236,880	
Expenses:	($97,645)	-38.7%	($97,645)	-39%
Net Operating Income:	$96,647		$139,235	
Loan Payments:	($96,408)		($96,408)	
Pre-Tax Cash Flow[2]:	$239	0.1%	$42,827	22.1%
Principal Reduction:	$13,532		$13,532	
Total Return[2]:	$13,770	7.1%	$56,358	29.1%

[1] As a percent of Scheduled Gross Income
[2] As a percent of Down Payment.

Scheduled Income			CURRENT RENTS		MARKET RENTS		Estimated Expenses	
No. of Units	Bdrms/ Baths	Approx Sq. Ftg.	Monthly Rent/Unit ($)	Monthly Income ($)	Monthly Rent/Unit ($)	Monthly Income ($)	Taxes	$37,975
							Insurance	$18,140
							Utilities	$0
20	3+3	1,265	1,050	21,000	1,050	21,000	Gardener	$6,000
							Maint./Repairs	$10,080
							Off-Site Mgr.	$15,120
							Advertising	$250
							Misc/Reserves	$10,080
								$97,645
Total Scheduled Rent:			$21,000		$21,000			
Laundry:			$0		$0			
Other Income:			$0		$0			
Monthly Scheduled Gross Income:			$21,000		$21,000		Total Expenses:	$97,645
Annualized Scheduled Gross Income:			$252,000		$252,000		Per Net Sq. Ft.:	$3.86
Utilities Paid by Tenant:		All utilities					Per Unit:	$4,882.25

As you may have guessed, scenarios rarely happen like this. If rental rates are falling, local vacancy rates are probably rising, and vice versa. This is not always the case and depends on the local economic factors contributing to the problem. In LA County, the rental market is very tight and the local vacancy factor hovers around 3%. In many parts of Texas and throughout the United States, the local vacancy factor is closer to 8%-12% historically. In these areas, overbuilding can cause an increase in supply, which lowers rental rates and possibly increases vacancy rates if there isn't enough demand to absorb all the new units available.

In doing your break-even analysis, it's wise to tinker with both the rental rate and vacancy rate at the same time. If rents were to fall to $950/month and the local vacancy rate rises closer to the historical norm of 12%, your Pre-Tax Cash Flow would go from $42,827 a year to $9,947 a year. You'd still be able to make your mortgage and expense payments, but you'd lose over 70% of your cash-on-cash return.

Property Address:			Texas Dupluxes
			Small Town, Texas

Summary		Current Rents	Market Rents	Proposed Financing		
Price:		$1,550,000		First Loan Amount: $1,395,000		New
Down Payment:	10%	$193,750		Terms: 5.75%		30 yr fixed
Number of Units:		20				
Cost per Unit:		$77,500				
Current GRM:		6.80	6.15	*Brand new construction.		
Current CAP:		6.9%	9.2%	*10 duplexes.		
Year Built / Age:		2004		*$125/month PMI payment.		
Approx. Lot Size:		74,750				
Approx. Net RSF:		25,300				
Cost per Net RSF:		$61				

Annualized Operating Data					
	Current Rents			Market Rents	
Scheduled Gross Income:	$228,000			$252,000	
Vacancy Rate Reserve[1]:	($27,360)	12.0%		($15,120)	6.0%
Gross Operating Income:	$200,640			$236,880	
Expenses:	($94,285)	-41.4%		($94,285)	-37%
Net Operating Income:	$106,355			$142,595	
Loan Payments:	($96,408)			($96,408)	
Pre-Tax Cash Flow[2]:	$9,947	5.1%		$46,187	23.8%
Principal Reduction:	$13,532			$13,532	
Total Return[2]:	$23,478	12.1%		$59,718	30.8%

[1] As a percent of Scheduled Gross Income
[2] As a percent of Down Payment.

Scheduled Income			CURRENT RENTS		MARKET RENTS		Estimated Expenses	
No. of Units	Bdrms/ Baths	Approx Sq. Ftg.	Monthly Rent/Unit ($)	Monthly Income ($)	Monthly Rent/Unit ($)	Monthly Income ($)	Taxes	$37,975
							Insurance	$18,140
							Utilities	$0
20	3+3	1,265	950	19,000	1,050	21,000	Gardener	$6,000
							Maint./Repairs	$9,120
							Off-Site Mgr.	$13,680
							Advertising	$250
							Misc/Reserves	$9,120
								$94,285
Total Scheduled Rent:			$19,000		$21,000			
Laundry:			$0		$0			
Other Income:			$0		$0			
Monthly Scheduled Gross Income:			$19,000		$21,000		Total Expenses:	$94,285
Annualized Scheduled Gross Income:			$228,000		$252,000		Per Net Sq. Ft.:	$3.73
Utilities Paid by Tenant:	All utilities						Per Unit:	$4,714.25

As you now realize, when considering an investment, it's important that you model different scenarios to understand the impact they may have on your expected outcome. The biggest factors investors are required to make assumptions about are: Vacancy Factor, Annual Rent Increase, Disposition CAP Rate, and Annual Expense Increase.

When creating a Cash Flow worksheet that stretches two years or more into the future, it's difficult to know with great certainty, how each of these factors will turn out (unless of course, you have a crystal ball). For example, you may assume that rents will increase by 4% annually over the next 10 years; but what if you're wrong, and they only increase by 3%? And, if rents only increase by 3%, does that mean the local vacancy rate is lower since rental rates are holding steady and tenants are less inclined to leave and look for cheaper housing? I suggest you model 3-5 scenarios that you consider *likely* to occur, or you could foresee occurring, at least some part of the time.

Below is a Sensitivity Analysis I did on a deal a client was looking to purchase. We wanted to find out what would happen if our Rent Increase projection was incorrect. In order to do this, we needed to keep all other variables constant. Remember, to change any of these variables, you just refer to the Excel spreadsheet and change the value in the corresponding cell. In this case, the Rent Increase variable is found on your Cash Flow worksheet. Changing it will change your IRR, and you want to record the IRR that corresponds to the appropriate Rent Increase.

Rent Increase Variable					
	#1	#2	#3	#4	#5
Rent Increases	3.0%	4.0%	5.0%	6.0%	7.0%
Expense Increase	1.5%	1.5%	1.5%	1.5%	1.5%
Vacancy Rate	3.0%	3.0%	3.0%	3.0%	3.0%
Disposition Cap Rate	6.5%	6.5%	6.5%	6.5%	6.5%
IRR	20.1%	22.9%	25.5%	28.0%	30.4%
Increase		2.8%	2.6%	2.5%	2.4%
% Increase		13.9%	11.4%	9.8%	8.6%

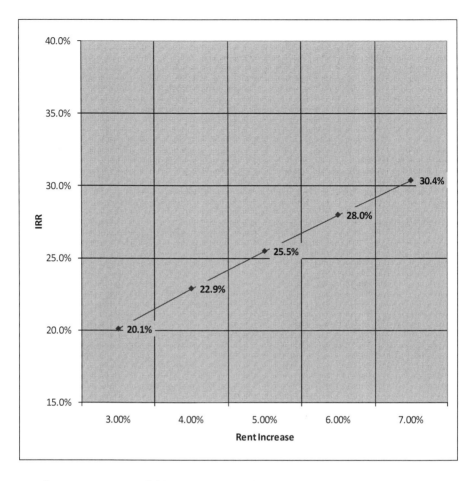

As you can see, I highlighted the Rent Increase and IRR rows. The only variable we tested for and changed was the Rent Increase Variable where we went from 3.0% up to 7.0%. As we did this, the IRR of the investment increased accordingly. This should make intuitive sense. If rents are increasing annually, two things will happen: First, your cash-on-cash return will grow at a quicker pace and you'll have more spendable income each year; and second, your NOI will increase faster and will be greater at the time of sale. Since the value of the property is calculated using the NOI at time of sale, the greater the NOI, the greater the property value. Remember, we're keeping the Disposition CAP Rate constant (in this case at 6.5%). For example, the value of property at a 6.0% CAP with a $1MM NOI is $16.67MM, calculated as follows:

Property Value = NOI/CAP Rate = $1MM/.06 = $16.67MM

Let's assume rents grew by 3% annually over the hold period rather than 7%, resulting in an NOI of $900,000 instead of $1MM. In this case, the property would only be worth $15MM at a 6.0% CAP, or $1.67MM less. As you can see illustrated above, increasing the annual rent growth rate from 3% to 4% increases your IRR from 20.1% to 22.9%, which is a 14% increase. You can perform similar calculations for each of the factors above.

Next is a chart/graph I created to see how the Disposition CAP Rate affected the overall IRR of a deal. Again, the only row that I changed is highlighted. In each of the five scenarios, I kept all other variables constant except for the Disposition CAP Rate. As you can see, the Disposition CAP Rate also has a significant effect on your IRR. If you guesstimated wrong and thought your Disposition CAP Rate was going to be 6.0% instead of 6.5%, your IRR would fall from 22.2% to 20.1%, which is a 9.5% decrease in value, calculated as follows:

22.2% - 20.1% = 2.1%/22.2% = 9.5% decrease

Disposition Cap Rate Variable					
	#1	#2	#3	#4	#5
Rent Increase	3.0%	3.0%	3.0%	3.0%	3.0%
Expense Increase	1.5%	1.5%	1.5%	1.5%	1.5%
Vacancy Rate	3.0%	3.0%	3.0%	3.0%	3.0%
Disposition Cap Rate	5.5%	6.0%	6.5%	7.0%	7.5%
IRR	24.5%	22.2%	20.1%	18.0%	16.1%
Increase/Decrease	2.3%	2.1%		-2.1%	-1.9%
% +/-	10.4%	10.4%		-10.4%	-10.6%

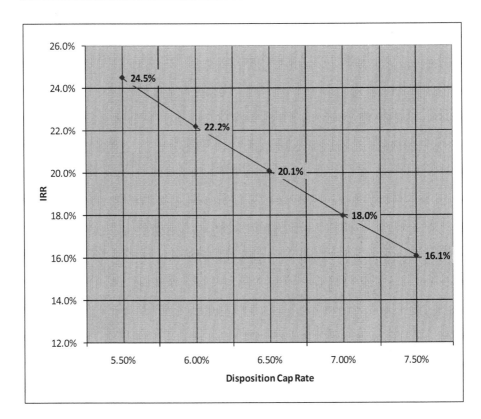

Now that you've tested for individual factors, it's time to test for multiple factors. In the real world, shifts never happen alone. Usually, if one variable moves, so will another. For example, if rental rates rise, expenses will also; and as you're now familiar with, rising rental rates usually signals an inflationary period.

Below is a chart that contains five scenarios that I've imagined might occur over any investment period. You're free to change these as you like or create your own. For example, if you're buying a single tenant NNN deal (like a Walgreen's or McDonald's), there's little need to model any scenario except a change to the Disposition CAP Rate since your income stream is guaranteed by a long-term lease with pre-set rental increases.

Expected Return

	Expected Scenario	Better than expected rent increase	Brisk rent increase, increased CPI, increased expenses	Slow rent increases, higher vacancy, lower resale value	Slow rent increases, higher vacancy	
Rent Increase	4.0%	5.0%	7.0%	3.0%	3.0%	
Expense Increase	1.5%	2.0%	2.5%	2.0%	2.0%	
Vacancy Rate	3.0%	3.0%	2.0%	5.0%	5.0%	
Disposition Cap Rate	6.5%	6.5%	7.0%	7.5%	6.5%	
IRR	22.9%	25.4%	28.6%	15.9%	19.8%	
Expected Probability	35%	20%	20%	10%	15%	100%
Expected Return	23.4%					

What follows are my thoughts on each scenario represented in this table. Note that I've highlighted the cells in bold font that vary from the Expected Scenario.

Expected Scenario - This is what I expect (to occur) the majority of the time.

Better-than-expected rent increase - In this scenario, rents increase at a 5.0% annual rate rather than 4.0%. Also, since we're likely in an inflationary period of escalating rents, I assume my expenses increase at a 2.0% annual rate versus 1.5%.

Brisk rent increase, increased CPI, increased expenses - Here, I assume rents rapidly increase at 7.0%, with a corresponding 2.5% expense increase. Also, since rents are increasing so rapidly, this probably signals an increased demand which leads to a lower vacancy rate. If rents are increasing so rapidly, it may be due to the lack of available for-sale housing usually signaled by higher interest rates. After all, people usually rent when they can't afford to buy; and, high interest rates result in higher mortgage payments and lower affordability. If interest rates *have* increased, so have CAP Rates since interest rates generally move in lock step with CAP Rates, increasing and falling together.

Slow rent increases, higher vacancy, lower resale value - This scenario is more of a doomsday scenario where rents escalate more slowly and local vacancy is high. This might occur in an area where overbuilding has occurred and there's more supply than demand (refer back to the Texas Example). In this case, you'd see slow rent growth and higher vacancy levels. To make matters worse, I've assumed my Disposition CAP Rate is far higher than my Expected

Scenario, meaning my property value will be much lower at time of sale; hence, the lower IRR for this scenario.

Slow rent increases, higher vacancy - This scenario is similar to the one above; however, the Disposition CAP Rate does not move, so the property value at time of sale is not negatively affected.

Once you've defined your different scenarios and calculated the corresponding IRRs, you need to assign a *probability* to each. This is, basically, the likelihood you believe of that scenario occurring. In my example, I believe the Expected Scenario will occur 35% of the time, and the second scenario will occur 20% of the time. It's important to make sure the sum of your projected percentages totals to 100%, no more and no less. Remember, some of these scenarios are very unlikely; but, your goal in doing this exercise is to account for the unexpected.

Your final step is to solve for your Expected Return. Excel can do this for you; and the formula you use is below.

Expected Return = IRR of Scenario #1*Probability of Scenario#1 + IRR of Scenario #2*Probability of Scenario#2.... +IRR of Scenario #5*Probability of Scenario #5

In this example, the Expected Return is an IRR of 23.9%. This falls in the middle of the individual IRRs for each scenario, which range from 15.9% to 28.6%. This should make sense because if your Expected Return for this example came back at 29.2%, you'd know something was miscalculated since there is no way your Expected Return could exceed any of the individual IRRs.

I like using an Expected Return versus an individual IRR. It's a more robust calculation and accounts for any errors I might make on some of my assumptions. Obviously, there's no guarantee that your probabilities are correct or that your scenarios will occur. The point is that you've spent time critically thinking through all possibilities and you've made an attempt to account for them so you're prepared for the unexpected.

As a start, go ahead and use the five scenarios I've outlined. However, as you discuss the Sensitivity Analysis with your agent, partner(s), and other local investors, you'll probably come up with other scenarios you feel are more relevant to your particular investment. In that case, replace mine with yours to make the analysis as robust and complete as possible. The most important thing is to think through each scenario and make sure it makes economic sense.

CHAPTER 10 — TAXES & DEPRECIATION: ACCOUNTING FOR YOUR SILENT PARTNER, UNCLE SAM

In the real world, your silent partner, Uncle Sam, is going to want his share of your income each year in the form of taxes. Since there's no legal way around paying taxes, this chapter discusses how to account for them and the implications they have on your investment decisions. Remember, I'm not a tax professional and the information provided here is purely for educational purposes. You should consult with your tax professional to make sure you are adhering to the law.

In order to create a realistic view of any investment, we need to incorporate taxes and *depreciation* into the equation. Depreciation is a term used to describe the fact that assets lose value over time and eventually become worthless. For example, a 20-year-old car has almost no value in the marketplace since it's worn out and most likely no longer in working condition. Real estate is the same since over time, properties become *tired*, worn out, and often need repair in the form of updated plumbing, electric, paint, and new roofing.

Because of this, the government allows you to take a deduction called *Depreciation Expense* each year you own the property. It's based on a set schedule and varies by property type. For multi-family property, you're allowed to deduct this expense over the *useable life* of the asset, which is deemed to be 27.5 years; and for commercial property, it's 39 years. What this means is that each year, for 27.5 years, the government allows you to deduct a Depreciation Expense based on the value of your property at the time of purchase. The only caveat is that you subtract the value of the land from the total value of the property since land does not depreciate (lose value over time). This is called the *Improvement Value* of a property, and refers to the value of the *structures* on the parcel of land. Every property that has Improvements on it derives its value from two sources: The value of the land and the value of the Improvements on the land (for example, a 10-unit multi-family building).

In order to figure out what your annual Depreciation Expense allowance is, the first thing you want to do is calculate the Improvement Value. You can do this a number of different ways. First, you can ask your accountant to help you by providing him with a copy of your Closing Statement. Second, you can visit the local Tax Assessor's Office and find out what ratio they're using for the value of land versus improvements. Many tax statements even show this. For example, on one of my properties, the purchase price was $3MM; but the Assessor values the improvements at $1.8MM, or 60% of the purchase price. In this case, the Improvement Value is 60%. Third, you can engage the services of an appraiser to value the land and property separately.

The most important thing is that if you get audited by the IRS, you can provide them with documentation substantiating how you arrived at the Improvement Value you used to set your Depreciation Schedule. It would be very difficult for you to prove your Improvement Value should be 100% since that would mean the land is worthless, which the government probably won't agree with.

The Improvement Value of your property can change over time. If you add a new roof or upgrade the plumbing, you've increased the value of the improvements, and these Capital expenditures are depreciable. When you spend money on Capital expenditures, you want to provide your accountant with receipts so he can set up a depreciation schedule based on the monies spent and the type of improvement. Depreciation schedules are usually based on the useful life of an improvement and can range from 5 years to 27.5 years. For example, a new roof with a 15-year useful life would be depreciated over 15 years, while new plumbing might be depreciated over 27.5 years. Your accountant will consult an IRS guide to determine the exact useful life. Conversely, the Improvement Value of your property can decline if damages occur that are not repaired, such as from fire or some other casualty of nature.

Below is a worksheet that incorporates both Taxes and Depreciation. This is based on a 25-unit apartment complex in LA County, purchased for $3.6MM with $1.15MM down (including closing costs). The investor took out a 5-year fixed loan with Interest-Only payments for the full 5-year term. I assume that in Year 6 the investor will do a cash-out refinance into another 5-year fixed loan with fully-amortized payments. The property's improvement value is estimated at 70%, and a 27.5 year straight-line depreciation schedule is used. Finally, the investor's tax rate is assumed to be 40%. This worksheet is the same as the other Cash Flow worksheets we've used before, with the addition of a few new rows.

Depreciation/Taxes Cash Flow Worksheet										
Purchase Price	$ 3,600,000									
Initial Equity Investment Yr 1	$1,150,000									
Improvement Value	70%									
Depreciation Period	27.5 years									
Income Tax Rate	40%									
	Year 1	Year 2	Year 3	Year 4	Year 5	Year 6	Year 7	Year 8	Year 9	Year 10
Scheduled Gross Income:	$325,620	$338,645	$352,191	$366,278	$380,929	$396,167	$412,013	$428,494	$445,633	$463,459
Vacancy Rate Reserve:	($9,769)	($10,159)	($10,566)	($10,988)	($11,428)	($11,885)	($12,360)	($12,855)	($13,369)	($13,904)
Gross Operating Income:	$315,851	$328,485	$341,625	$355,290	$369,501	$384,282	$399,653	$415,639	$432,264	$449,555
Estimated Expenses:	($114,734)	($116,455)	($118,202)	($119,975)	($121,774)	($123,601)	($125,455)	($127,337)	($129,247)	($131,186)
Net Operating Income:	$201,117	$212,030	$223,423	$235,315	$247,727	$260,680	$274,198	$288,302	$303,017	$318,369
Loan Payments:	($148,800)	($148,800)	($148,800)	($148,800)	($148,800)	(217,234)	($217,234)	($217,234)	($217,234)	($217,234)
Pre-Tax Cash Flow:	$52,317	$63,230	$74,623	$86,515	$98,927	$43,447	$56,964	$71,068	$85,784	$101,136
Less Depreciation	($91,636)	($91,636)	($91,636)	($91,636)	($91,636)	($91,636)	($91,636)	($91,636)	($91,636)	($91,636)
Plus Principal Reduction	$0	$0	$0	$0	$0	$28,368	$29,368	$30,368	$31,368	$32,368
Taxable Income	($39,319)	($28,406)	($17,013)	($5,121)	$7,291	($19,822)	($5,305)	$9,800	$25,515	$41,867
Less Income Taxes	($15,728)	($11,362)	($6,805)	($2,049)	$2,916	($7,929)	($2,122)	$3,920	$10,206	$16,747
After Tax Income	$68,045	$74,593	$81,428	$88,564	$96,011	$51,375	$59,086	$67,148	$75,578	$84,389

Negative Income Tax Due can either offset other passive/active income or be carried forward as Net Operating Loss	
Annual Rent Increase	4.00%
Annual Expense Increase	1.50%
Year 5 Refi to payoff Seller 1st TD and put a permanent loan in place	
Expected NOI	$260,680
Expected DCR	1.20
Expected Interest Rate	6.50%
Maximum Debt Service	$ 217,234
Maximum Loan Amount	$ 2,836,784
Equity In Deal	$ 763,216
Equity Returned	$386,784

Once we dip below the Pre-Tax Cash Flow row you'll notice some new entries. The first is Less Depreciation. Depreciation is a *non-cash expense* you're allowed to deduct annually from your Pre-Tax Cash Flow. It's a non-cash expense because you're not paying this amount to anyone, but you're deducting it from your income. In this example, the annual depreciation allowance is equal to $91,636, calculated as follows:

Depreciation Allowance = (Purchase Price*Improvement Value)/27.5
= ($3.6MM*.7)/27.5

Notice this amount does not vary from year to year. The only time it varies is if you own the property for less than 12 months, or purchase or sell in the middle of a year. In that case, your accountant will calculate your exact allowance for that period.

The next line item is *Plus Principal Reduction*. Principal Reduction is the portion of your monthly mortgage payment that goes towards paying down the principal balance on your loan. On a 30-year loan you have an amortization period that stretches for 30 years. Each year, some portion of your payment goes toward paying down your loan, and this amount increases over time.

In this example, the investor is making Interest-Only loan payments in Years 1-5. There's no money going towards paying down the principal, so the Principal Reduction figure is $0. When the loan is refinanced in Year 6, the investor plans on taking out a fully-amortized loan which requires some part of the monthly payment go towards Principal Reduction. At that point, this figure goes from being $0 to whatever the annual amount is that you're paying down (in this example the figure is $28,368). You can estimate this figure with a mortgage calculator or by creating an amortization schedule in Excel. Also, your lender will send you a 1099 for Interest Expense every year (sometime in early February), and this indicates exactly how much you paid in Interest and Principal in the preceding year.

The next line item is *Taxable Income*. This figure is obtained using the following calculation:

Taxable Income = Pre-Tax Cash Flow - Depreciation + Principal Reduction

Remember, depreciation is an *allowable expense*, so you subtract it from your Pre-Tax Cash Flow. Principal Reduction is *not* an allowable expense. While the government allows you to deduct the interest you pay on your mortgage as an expense, you cannot deduct the portion of your payment that goes towards principal reduction, and this must be added back to your Pre-Tax Cash Flow.

The next line item is *Less Income Taxes*. This is a simple calculation, as follows:

Income Taxes = Tax Rate * Taxable Income

In our example, the investor's tax rate is 40%. Notice in the first few years of ownership, the Income Tax figure is negative ($15,728 in Year 1). This means the investor does not owe any taxes, and that he has a credit due from the IRS. This Net Operating Loss, or NOL as it's referred to, can be carried over to another part of the investor's tax return. For example, if he owns another property he owes $22,000 in taxes on, he can offset that with the $15,728 loss he has on this property, for a net tax bill calculated as follows:

$22,000 - $15,728 = $6,278

The final line item is your *After Tax Income*. In Year 1 this amounts to $68,045, calculated as follows:

After Tax Income = Pre-Tax Cash Flow - Income Taxes =
$52,317 - ($15,728)

In some years where your Income Tax owed is a negative figure, your After Tax Income will be larger than your Taxable Income. Basically, you'll have a tax savings on some other part of your tax return due to your loss on an investment. As you can see, Depreciation is one of the great benefits of real estate ownership as it can shield a large portion of your annual income. In this example, the Depreciation Expense allowed is $91,636 per year, which lowers your Taxable Income to $0 or less in Years 1-7, meaning you will not owe any taxes in those years, and may have a refund coming.

Taxes can be quite complicated, but there are a few important rules that you should understand and discuss with your tax professional. The first is that most individuals who are not classified as *real estate professionals* are limited by the amount of Passive Losses they can deduct in any one year. A real estate professional is someone who works at least 750 hours per year in the real estate business such as brokerage, development, or management (you do not need to be a licensed real estate professional, but if audited, you will need to be able to document how your time is spent). Most investors do not qualify under these guidelines, so their losses and gains are considered *Passive*, not *Active*.

Further, the IRS limits your total Passive loss deduction to $25,000 a year. However, if you make $100,000 or more, this figures decreases on a sliding scale, until it reaches $0 for earners of $150,000 or more in a year. Essentially, if you make over $150,000 in one year and are not considered a real estate professional, you cannot deduct any Passive losses on your tax return. That being said, you can use passive losses incurred in the operating of your rental properties to offset passive gains made elsewhere. Some of my clients use their passive real estate losses to offset large passive gains earned in their stock and bond portfolio.

Now, if you're able to classify yourself as a real estate professional under the IRS's guidelines, you're not subject to the same $25,000 limit. In fact, you can deduct all of your income property losses against any income you make in that year. One of my colleagues is a successful real estate broker and property owner who generates over $500,000 per year in brokerage commission income *and* he owns over 100 units in LA County. Those properties generated a $125,000 loss in 2006, and he was able to offset his taxable income by that same amount, owing taxes on $375,000 instead of $500,000.

My suggestion is to always consult your tax professional before making any Buy or Sell decision. You want to fully explore the ramifications of all decisions and understand what the tax implications will be since, for example, the government taxes you at different rates based on the length of time you hold an investment. Two such designations are noted below.

Short-Term Gains - Usually, any investment held for less than 12 months will be taxed as Short-Term Capital Gains or Ordinary Income. This is a much higher rate for most people and can come close to 48% or more if you live in California.

Long-Term Gains - Usually, any investment held for more than 12 months will be taxed as Long-Term Capital Gains. The current Federal rate is 15%. There's continuing debate in Congress as to whether this rate should be increased; but as of 2008, it stood at 15%. You should speak with your accountant about your specific investment tax consequences as some long-term projects, such as condo conversions, may be subject to Ordinary Income taxes depending upon the type of entity that held title and how the project was managed.

As you can see, it's often advantageous to hold a property for 13 months instead of 12 since you end up paying Long -Term Capital Gains instead of Short-Term Capital Gains. This can amount to a savings of 15%-20% or more, depending upon your situation.

CHAPTER 11 — HOW TO TAKE TITLE: WHAT'S THE RIGHT OWNERSHIP ENTITY FOR ME?

O nce you decide to purchase a property, you need to figure out the best way to take title. There are many options available and each has its pros and cons. I've provided an explanation of the benefits of each, and associated costs, if any. Again, you want to discuss these options with your tax professional and attorney to determine which one is best for you.

Ownership as an Individual - If you're buying the property without any partners, you may consider taking title as an individual. Many people take ownership of their homes in this manner, and some investors use this method as well; but it's become less popular with the advent of the LLC (Limited Liability Company). When you take title as an individual, all losses and gains automatically flow through to your tax return in the year they're realized.

If you want to purchase a property with a partner(s) and take title as *individuals*, you can create an arrangement known as *Joint Tenancy* or *Tenants-in-Common*. Joint Tenancy is where all individuals on title have equal ownership of the property. If there are two partners, each owns 50%. If there are three partners, each owns 33-1/3%. Additionally, when one of the joint tenants dies, his/her interest automatically goes to the surviving joint tenant(s) rather than to the deceased's heirs. Because of this, Joint Tenancy is usually best for family members and husband/wife situations rather than business partners.

Tenants-in-Common is similar to Joint Tenancy; however, the individuals on title need not own an *equal* share. For example, if you had three partners, one could own 50%, another 30%, and the final partner could own 20%. Like Joint Tenancy, each individual's name would appear on the title, such as Sally Q. Jones and Jerry T. Smith.

It's advisable that anytime you purchase property with a partner, you have an *Operating Agreement* in place detailing how you intend to operate the property and what steps need to be taken in the case of a sale or liquidation.

Corporate Ownership - Unlike Individual Ownership, corporations are taxable entities which means they must file a separate tax return annually on all profits/losses made. Then, any proceeds can be distributed to shareholders who, in turn, must pay their individual taxes. This double-taxation scenario has made this type of ownership somewhat unpopular; however, there are some advantages to taking ownership in this way. First, shareholders have limited liability and *do not* have any more Capital at risk than they have invested in the project. If you invested $50,000 in an investment, you cannot lose more than that amount, even if the investment were to go bankrupt. Second, corporate shares can easily be sold and traded much more readily than real property. Third, corporate shares are easier to transfer upon death and inheritance than real property.

General Partnerships - These entities were very popular a few years back due to the fact they're *not* taxable entities, unlike corporations. Each Partner receives his/her pro rata share of all gains and losses which automatically flows to the individual's tax return. One of the disadvantages of this ownership structure is the *unlimited liability* every Partner shares. For example, if you were to invest $50,000 and the investment went bankrupt, you could be personally liable for far more than your original investment. As a result, this ownership structure has lost popularity in favor of the LLC.

Limited Partnerships - LPs are a viable alternative to General Partnerships in that they limit an investor's personal liability to the amount of his investment, and do not have the double taxation associated with Corporate Ownership. Usually, a General Partner(s) handles the day-to-day management of the investment; and this individual(s) has unlimited liability for partnership obligations, even though the Limited Partners do not. Due to the current tax climate, this ownership structure has fallen out of favor as well.

Limited Liability Company - LLCs have become the ownership vehicle of choice for most real estate investors since they combine the tax advantages of the Limited Partnership with the limited liability advantages of the Corporation. All members of the LLC, including the Managing Member(s), have limited liability to the extent of their

147

investment. Additionally, if structured properly, LLCs are treated as a pass-through entity by the IRS, meaning that each member receives their pro rata share of gains and losses which flows directly to their individual tax returns.

It's important to note that some of the ownership entities listed here have tax consequences above and beyond what you may be accustomed to. For instance, in many states you need to file a separate tax return for an LLC. In California, you have a minimum $800 fee to the state, plus any costs incurred for your accountant to prepare the return. The benefits LLCs provide often outweigh these costs, but you want to carefully review everything ahead of time. Finally, you want to decide early in your escrow period, and while you're applying for your loan, how you'll take title. The lender will want to know, and there may be some additional paperwork required depending on the ownership structure you decide on.

CHAPTER 12 – 1031 EXCHANGES: DO I REALLY HAVE TO PAY TAXES???

One of the most powerful tools at your disposable as a real estate investor is the Tax Deferred 1031 Exchange. This "tax loophole" lets you defer paying taxes on gains from a sale to sometime in the future. Investors and families have used 1031s to defer taxes for years and even decades, passing the property on from one generation to the next. Many experts define a 1031 Exchange as follows:

An otherwise taxable gain realized on an exchange of like-kind assets need not be recognized in the year of the transaction. Tax liability is postponed until a future, taxable transaction occurs with respect to the newly acquired property.

1031 Exchanges are one of the keys to successfully building your portfolio and amassing a real estate empire. Well, maybe not an empire, but whatever goals you set for yourself. In this chapter, I'm going to show you how a 1031 Exchange works and explain the basics. Remember, however, it's imperative you consult with your tax professional before buying or selling any property. A 1031 Exchange has long-term tax ramifications; and you should fully investigate these with your accountant before making any investment decisions. I'm not an accountant, and you probably are not one either. As an investor, you want to work with an accountant who's familiar with real estate and 1031 Exchanges and can help guide you through the process.

Why do a 1031 Exchange. To encourage real estate investment and ownership, the U.S. government created Section 1031 of the Internal Revenue Code which defines the rules and guidelines for a Tax-Deferred Exchange. Basically, these rules allow you to sell a property today and defer the taxes due on the gain until sometime in the future as long as you comply with the letter of the law.

The example I'm about to share follows a client of mine who purchased a 12-unit property for $1.25MM and held it for 5 years. Upon sale, it was valued at $2.5MM and he had a decision to make: Should he do a 1031 Exchange and use the proceeds to purchase another property or should he pay taxes? And if he were to do a 1031 Exchange, what would the total monetary benefit, or tax savings, be? As you'll see below, my client's total tax liability if he opted to forgo a 1031 Exchange, would be $321,868 distributed between federal and CA state taxes (based on 2008 tax rates). If my client did a 1031 Exchange, he could defer that tax payment sometime into the future and have use of those funds now. If he were to invest that $321,868 at a 16% IRR over a 20-year period, it would grow to over $6.2MM. So by doing a 1031 Exchange, my client would generate an additional $6.2MM in value over the next 20 years.

Hold Period	5 years
Purchase Price	1,250,000
Sales Price	2,500,000
Less Sale Costs (6.0%)	(150,000)
Less Debt	1,000,000
Net Proceeds	1,350,000
Depreciation*	159,091
Taxable Gain on Sale	1,259,091
1031 Debt to Replace	1,000,000
1031 Equity to Replace	1,350,000
Gain on Sale due to Depreciation	159,091
Gain on Sale due to Appreciation	1,100,000
Taxes due to Depreciation Recapture	54,568
Taxes due to Capital Gain on Sale	267,300
Total Taxes due	321,868
Percentage of Taxes/Total Gain	25.6%
Tax Savings due to 1031 Exchange	**321,868**
Investment Rate	16.00%
Investment Period	20
Value of Tax Savings over Investment Period	**6,263,799**

*Based on 70% improvement value and 27.5 years Straight Line Depreciation
**Assume 9.3% CA state tax

What I want to do is walk you through this example step-by-step as I know it can seem daunting and complicated for many who are not comfortable with math. The key to understanding 1031 Exchanges is not being great at math, but actually understanding how each line item was arrived at. Someone else can help you create this table, but you want to at least be able to comprehend it.

Step 1: The hold period in this example was 5 years. My client purchased the property in 2000, for $1.25MM (taking out a $1MM loan), and we listed it for sale in 2005, for $2.5MM. The total depreciation he expensed on his tax return over the 5-year period was $159,091. This was based on a 70% improvement value and a 27.5-year straight-line depreciation schedule. What that means is that he was valuing the improvements on the land (the building) at 70% of the purchase price. In this case, 70% of $1.25MM is $875,000. This amount was then depreciated equally over 27.5 years, which comes out to $31,818 each year in depreciation expense.

Step 2: Once we listed the property for sale at $2.5MM and received some offers, my client decided to go ahead with the sale. The total sale costs were 6.0% which were comprised of title/escrow fees, city and county transfer taxes, real estate brokerage commissions, and some other small charges. These costs totaled $150,000. Upon sale, my client was left with $1.35MM. This was the balance after we subtracted the sale costs of $150,000 and the existing mortgage balance of $1MM from the $2.5MM sale price (he had an interest-only loan, so the principal balance did not change).

Step 3: The most important step in this process was to decide whether or not to proceed with a 1031 Exchange; so, we needed to calculate how much my client's tax liability would be to determine whether or not it was worth deferring the gain and taxes. My client's tax liability was composed of two parts: Depreciation recapture and appreciation. The first component, depreciation recapture, is taxed at a 25% federal rate, plus whatever the local tax rate was (in this case, it was 9.3% in the state of California). We simply took 34.3% (25% + 9.3%) of the $159,091 he subtracted throughout the 5-year hold period for depreciation. This totaled $54,568. That was his total tax liability due to depreciation recapture.

Next, we needed to calculate what his tax liability would be due to the gain on the sale. To do this we first had to compute what the gain on the sale was. In this case, the gain was equal to the sale price

($2.5MM) less the selling costs ($150,000), less the depreciation expensed during the hold period ($159,091), less the original purchase price of the property ($1.25MM). That totals $1.1MM and is equal to the total gain on the sale due to appreciation. Since this property was held for 5 years, the gain was considered a Long-Term Capital Gain and taxed at a 15% federal rate, plus whatever the local state rate was (in this case, 9.3% for CA). The total tax liability equaled 24.3% of the $1.1MM gain or $267,300.

The total tax liability due, if my client opted to forgo a 1031 Exchange, would be the $54,568 for the depreciation recapture, plus $267,300 for the Capital gain, for a total of $321,868. That means that if my client did NOT do a 1031 Exchange, he would owe the government, between state and federal, a total of $321,868 in taxes. This amount represented almost 26% of his total gain on the property, which is calculated by dividing the $321,868 tax liability into the $1,259,091 total gain.

Every time you sell a piece of property you will have two gains from the sale. One gain will be due to the depreciation you expensed during ownership and the other gain will be due to appreciation. You will always have the first gain because every year you own a property, you expense depreciation and this lowers your cost basis until you finally run out of depreciation, which takes 27.5 years on a multi-family property. In the government's eyes, once you lower the cost basis of a property, you have a gain. In this example, you're lowering the cost basis by $31,818 per year; so if you had no gain that year due to appreciation, you'd still have a gain of $31,818 due to depreciation.

The second gain, from appreciation, may or may not occur. It depends on whether you sell your property for more than you bought it. In fact, it's a little more complicated than that. The government allows you to lower your cost basis by subtracting the costs of sale (title/escrow fees, brokerage fees, etc.). In my example above, the sale costs were $150,000. Let's assume that you bought the property for $2.4MM instead of $1.25MM. The government's viewpoint is that you would NOT have a gain on the sale due to appreciation. According to them, you would realize a $50,000 loss, as calculated below:

Sale Price	$2,500,000
Less Sale Costs	$ 150,000
Less Purchase Price	$2,400,000
Gain	($ 50,000)

What most people don't realize is that while you can expense depreciation every year and take it as a write-off, *eventually* you're going to need to repay those monies. The government will allow you to postpone repayment as long as you continue doing 1031 exchanges; but at some point, once you stop, you'll have a large tax bill.

The best way to think about this is like a loan. In my client's case, his federal tax rate was 38.3% and his CA tax rate was 9.3%. Each year he took a write-off for depreciation, he saved 48.6% on his taxes from the depreciation expense. When he finally sold a property and didn't do a 1031 Exchange, he had to repay all the depreciation he'd written off at 34.3% (25% federal plus 9.3% state). In essence, he saved 14.3% (48.6% - 34.3% = 14.3%). Again, the most important thing to remember is that eventually you will need to repay part of the monies you saved in the form of Depreciation Recapture. Don't be surprised by this; make sure you're prepared for it. If you've owned a property for many years and depreciated $1MM or more of value over the years, you'll have a tax bill in the $340,000 range, which is quite large, even if you did prepare for it.

My client, like most savvy real estate investors, decided that $321,000 was too large a sum to pay in taxes; so he decided to take that money, do a 1031 Exchange, and defer this tax payment to sometime into the future.

I know that for many people, the calculations I just covered seem quite complex. It doesn't have to be. You can and should lean on the advice of your tax professional to help you through these calculations. The calculations are reasonably straightforward and are important to help you decide which option to choose. In most cases where you have a significant gain, you want to do a 1031 Exchange. There are cases, however, where your gain might be more modest, and the best decision may well be to pay your taxes now and start fresh on your next investment. Only you can determine what this threshold amount will be; but, my advice is to use the example above to determine how much money that tax payment could grow into before you make your decision. As you see in our example, my client's $321,000 tax liability is projected to be worth over $6MM in 20 years. That's quite a large sum to almost anybody.

Now that you know why you would a 1031 Exchange, let's discuss how to do one. The first step to understanding a 1031 Exchange is to learn the basic parameters that govern them. Below is a list that you can refer back to.

- Property sold must have been held for *productive use* in a trade or business or an investment, and must be exchanged for *like-kind* property that is also to be used in a trade or business, or held as an investment.

- Property must be of like-kind.

- You must *replace* all debt and equity.

- You must identify your replacement property(ies) within *45 days* of close of escrow of your sale (relinquished) property.

- You must close escrow on the purchase of your replacement property(ies) *within 180 days* of close of escrow of your sale (relinquished) property.

- You may identify up to three replacement properties, or you may identify any number of replacement properties as long as their aggregate fair market value does not exceed 200 percent of the aggregate fair market value of your sale (relinquished) property. As a final option, you may identify any number of replacement properties as long as you acquire at least 95 percent of the aggregate fair market value of all the identified replacement property *within 180 days* of close of escrow of your sale (relinquished) property.

I realize the above list can seem daunting and complicated. Consult with your tax professional on these matters throughout the process. Another great resource is your *accommodator* who also assists you in this process. Accommodators are third-party intermediaries charged with escrowing your 1031 Exchange funds during your identification period (the period between when you close on your sale property and when you close on your replacement property). The fee charged for a 1031 Exchange typically ranges from $500-$1,000.

Here are a couple of website links to some accommodators or exchange companies (you can find many more by doing an Internet search). You'll find valuable information on these sites and greater detail about how 1031 Exchanges work.

www.downstreamexchange.com
www.1031exchange.com

Now that I've inundated you with the technical details on a 1031 Exchange, I want to explain it in laymen's terms. Here are the basics to get you started. First, the chart below details a 1031 Exchange I completed for one of my clients. It was somewhat complicated in that we sold three properties and replaced those with two others.

Sale (Relinquished) Properties

Adress	Sale Price	Debt	Sale Costs	Equity	Close Date
Apt. Building #1	4,100,000	759,000	141,000	3,200,000	1/17/2006
Apt. Building #2	3,900,000	1,106,000	134,000	2,660,000	12/15/2005
Apt. Building #3	4,600,000	1,022,000	228,000	3,350,000	12/30/2005
Total	12,600,000	2,887,000	503,000	9,210,000	

Purchase (Replacement) Properties

Address	Purchase Price	Debt	Closing Costs	Equity	Close Date
Single Tenant NNN Office	10,950,000	7,520,000	165,000	3,595,000	1/19/2006
Multi-Tenant Office	15,055,000	9,300,000	372,000	6,127,000	1/20/2006
Total	26,005,000	16,820,000	537,000	9,722,000	

DOES THIS MEET THE REQUIREMENTS OF A 1031 EXCHANGE?

New Debt exceeds old debt 16,820,000 > 2,787,000
New Equity exceeds old equity 9,722,000 > 9,210,000
Purchase Price exceeds sale price 26,005,000 > 12,600,000
All escrows closed within 180 days

In this example, my client sold three apartment buildings he'd owned for years. The aggregate value of those buildings at the time of sale was $12.6MM. There was a total of $2.887MM in existing debt (mortgages) at the time of sale, and the sale costs (title/escrow fees, real estate commissions, etc.) totaled $503,000. Upon close of escrow, my client had a total of $9.21MM in funds that he placed in an account with an accommodator. As you can see, all three properties were scheduled to close within 30 days of each other. This was done so that all proceeds could be used to exchange into larger properties at the same time.

Once available funds were on deposit with the accommodator, my client was ready to proceed with the purchase of the two replacement properties he chose to purchase: An office building costing $15MM and a single-tenant office property costing $10.9MM. Together they cost $26MM, which far exceeded the $12.6MM sale price of his three sale properties.

156

To purchase these two replacement properties, my client needed to originate new loans (debt) totaling $16.8MM, which far exceeded the $2.887MM in debt he had on his sale properties. The transactions required $9.7MM in equity, which used all $9.21MM in equity on deposit with the accommodator, plus another $500K in fresh Capital. Finally, both replacement property purchases were completed in mid-January, well within the 180-day requirement of the Internal Revenue Code.

As you can see, the above example meets all requirements of a 1031 Exchange. All of the equity proceeds from the sale were used (and even more in this case). The debt on the replacement properties was equal to or greater than the debt on the sale properties (much more, in this example). And, all replacement properties were purchased within the 180-day window. This is an example of a very successful 1031 Exchange. My client was able to sell $12.6MM worth of property and replace it with $26MM of property, which more than doubled his portfolio value.

It's important to note, my client not only used all of the equity from his sale properties, but also added fresh Capital to complete the purchase. A 1031 Exchange does not require you add fresh Capital, only that you use all of the equity you received from the sale. However, there are instances where you find you need to add fresh Capital due to the size and expense of your replacement property.

Below is a list I created to help summarize a 1031 Exchange. It's similar to the list above, but much less complicated. It should be referred to as a guide, but not as a definitive answer to all of your questions. You want to seek the advice of your tax professional for those questions that you're still unclear on.

- When you sell a property and do a 1031 Exchange, you must replace debt with debt and equity with equity. Simply, the total value of the mortgage(s) on your replacement property(ies) must be equal to or greater than the total debt on your sale property(ies). And, you must use all of the equity you received from your sale property(ies).

- You can NEVER take possession of the proceeds from your sale property(ies); and they must pass directly from your escrow company handling the sale straight to your accommodator. If you do handle the money, the exchange is no longer valid.

- You can sell multiple properties at or near the same time and use those funds to purchase one larger property or multiple properties, as long as you meet the financial and time requirements of a 1031 Exchange. This means you can sell 2 duplexes you own and use the proceeds to purchase a 10-unit building. Or, you can sell two 50-unit properties and use the proceeds to purchase four 30-unit buildings. As long as you replace all of the debt that existed on the sale properties and use all of the equity on deposit with your accommodator, you've met the requirements of a 1031 Exchange.

- Within 45 days of the close of escrow of your sale property(ies), you must identify *in writing* to your accommodator, what your anticipated replacement property(ies) is/are going to be. This is critical as it's necessary to have on file in the event of a tax audit. In fact, some accommodators require that you have this document notarized before you submit it.

- Finally, you must complete your exchange within 180 days of the close of your sale property. This is also critical as it results in an invalid exchange if it doesn't happen. It's one of the easiest things for the IRS to monitor, so be careful with regard to your timing. Most accommodators are mindful of the 45- and 180-day deadlines and will send you reminders as they approach; but you're wise to include this on your calendar.

1031 Exchanges are a great way for you to build your portfolio. I started with my first fourplex (valued at $280,000), and eventually grew that into a 23-unit apartment building (valued at over $3.5MM) through multiple 1031 Exchanges. One of the greatest benefits of real estate is your ability to defer the taxes on your gains into the future and use those funds to continue making money. Take advantage of this option whenever you can.

As I discussed in earlier chapters, you should regularly analyze your portfolio and make sure you're optimizing your equity. If you find your equity is not working to your maximum benefit, you have one of two options available: Do a cash-out refi and purchase more property, or do a 1031 Exchange and purchase a larger property. Either way, when you keep your equity working *for* you, your portfolio continues to grow and flourish.

CHAPTER 13 — THE PROPERTY LADDER: HOW TO BUILD YOUR OWN REAL ESTATE EMPIRE

You've probably heard of the concept called the Property Ladder on late-night TV, in another book, or on the Internet—and definitely in Chapter 1 of this book. It's a simple concept pertaining to real estate that basically says you purchase your first property then use that to purchase your next, and so on and so forth, until you've built a mini-empire. Conceptually, it's a brilliant idea that most investors employ, even if they don't realize what it's called. My investing career has involved moving up the Property Ladder as I described at the beginning of this book, starting with one fourplex, doing a 1031 Exchange into two others, and another 1031 Exchange into three more, all the way up to the purchase of a 23-unit multi-family property. That first fourplex cost $289,000 in 2002; and my most recent purchase was a 23-unit property costing $3.6MM in 2006, with many other properties and steps in between.

My personal story and Property Ladder journey happened to occur during one of the most vibrant and robust real estate markets of the last hundred years. In fact, property values and rents grew by an astronomical rate from 2001-2006, and many of my clients made millions during those years. Some of their success can be attributed to savvy investing, but a good part of it was due to luck and market timing. After all, no one predicted the market that occurred, and many LA County investors thought the market was peaking in 2003, which in retrospect couldn't have been more wrong.

The key to the Property Ladder is to keep your equity working. This is why I strongly urge you to regularly evaluate your portfolio every 6-12 months and review how your properties are doing, how much equity you've accrued, and make sure you're keeping pace with local rents. I always suggest to my clients that we regularly meet to review their holdings and see how they're doing. As their rental income grows, so does the value of their property and, in turn, the amount of equity in the property.

For example, let's assume you purchased a 10-unit multi-family property in 2003. At time of purchase, the monthly GSI was $15,000, and has since risen with annual rent increases to $17,000/month in 2005. The basic deal information is below:

# Units	10
Purchase Date	1/1/2003
Purchase Prie	1,800,000
LTV	70.0%
Interest Rate	6.00%
Loan Terms	5-yr fixed/ 5 y-yr I/O
Current GSI	$17,000/month
Current Expenses	$4,500/month
NOI	$12,500/month

Based on a 6.0% CAP, your property would be worth $2.5MM, calculated as follows:

Monthly NOI = $17,000 - $4,500 = $12,500
Annual NOI = $12,500*12 = $150,000
Property Value = NOI/CAP Rate = $150,000/.06 = $2,500,000

Let's assume that you raise rents by 5% in 2006, and your NOI increases from $150,000 to $157,500. Based on that same 6.0% CAP, your property value has increased to $2,625,000, and your equity has increased by $125,000.

As you know, most people don't own properties free and clear of debt. Let's assume in this example that you bought the property in 2003 for $1.8MM and put 30% down, or $540,000. In 2005, the value had risen to $2.5MM and in 2006, to $2.625MM. Your equity in the deal, in 2006, would now be $1,365,000, calculated as follows:

Original Equity = 30% Down = .3 * $1,800,000 = $540,000
Original Debt = 70% LTV = .7 * $1,800,000 = $1,260,000
Current Equity = Current Value - Existing Loan = $2,625,000 -
$1,260,000 = $1,365,000

Your total equity has increased from $540,000 to $1,365,000, or an increase of $825,000.

Note I'm assuming you've been making interest-only payments on the loan. If your loan payments were fully-amortized, you'd have paid your loan down some, and your equity would be slightly larger than $1,365,000.

Your Return on Investment (ROI), in 2006, would be 15.2%, calculated as follows:

$$NOI = \$157,500$$
$$Debt\ Service = \$1,260,000 * .06 = \$75,600$$
$$Pre\text{-}Tax\ Cash\ Flow = NOI - Debt\ Service = \$157,500 - \$75,600 = \$81,900$$
$$ROI = Pre\text{-}Tax\ Cash\ Flow/Down\ Payment = \$81,900/\$540,000 = 15.2\%$$

And, your Return on Equity (ROE) would be 6.0%, calculated as follows:

$$NOI = \$157,500$$
$$Debt\ Service = \$1,260,000 * .06 = \$75,600$$
$$Pre\text{-}Tax\ Cash\ Flow = \$157,500 - \$75,600 = \$81,900$$
$$ROE = Pre\text{-}Tax\ Cash\ Flow/Current\ Equity = \$81,900/\$1,365,000 = 6.0\%$$

Your ROI is your Pre-Tax Cash Flow divided by your initial down payment (plus closing costs) while your ROE is simply your Pre-Tax Cash Flow divided by the equity you have in the property at the time. Your ROI is always calculated using your initial down payment or invested funds; and this figure will never change since once you purchase a property, the amount you put down is static. That being said, if you were to do a cash-out refi, the amount you've invested would decrease by the amount of cash you pulled out. In the above example, your down payment will always be $540,000, unless you were to do a cash-out refi and pull out $200,000, in which case your total invested equity would decrease to $340,000; and that would be the new figure you'd use when calculating your ROI moving forward.

Your ROE, however, is a figure that's constantly in flux since your equity in the property is constantly in flux. In 2003 when the property was purchased, the down payment used would be equal to your equity. By 2006, this figure had changed and the equity in the property had grown to $1,365,000 or $825,000 more than the down payment.

When calculating your equity, it's important to understand that it's a somewhat academic figure. That's because there's no guarantee your property would sell for the value you've estimated it's worth. For example, in 2006, we estimated the above property was worth $2.625MM based on a 6.0% CAP. The 6.0% CAP was arrived at by looking at comparable sales and active listings in the market place. However, if the property were listed for sale in 2006, there's no guarantee it would sell for exactly $2.625MM, as it may sell for more and it may sell for less.

In the 10-unit example, the equity in the property had grown to $1,365,000 by 2006, and the ROE was falling; so, it was time for the owner to consider how he could unlock the equity gain and best put it to work for him. Usually, you have one of two options: You can sell the property and do a 1031 Exchange, or you can do a cash-out refi and use the cash to purchase another property. There's no right answer as to which option is best, and it varies by situation.

For example, if you spent a lot time and energy rehabbing this property, really liked the area and your tenants, and you thought there were even greater returns to be realized in the future, I'd recommend a cash-out refi. That being said, the first thing you should do is speak with a mortgage broker to find out how much money you could borrow by doing a cash-out refi, and what the rate and terms of the loan would be to help you make this decision.

Once you do a cash-out refi, your equity in the property decreases and your monthly debt service payments likely increase. First, your equity decreases because you're taking cash out. Second, your monthly debt service payments likely increase because you're replacing your current loan with a larger loan. Now, there are instances where this may not happen, for example, if interest rates have fallen enough that your interest payments don't increase.

Let's say you replaced a $1MM loan at 6.0% with a $1.2MM loan at 5.0%. In both cases, you'd have a $60,000 a year debt service payment, calculated as follows:

$$\$1MM * .06\% = \$60,000$$

$$\$1.2MM * .05\% = \$60,000$$

So, your Pre-Tax Cash Flow after you do a cash-out refi, will likely decrease, and in some rare instances, remain the same; but it will never increase. This should make intuitive sense since you're adding debt to the property that you have to service each month.

I'll walk you through both the sale/1031 Exchange and the cash-out refi options in more detail below.

OPTION 1 - SALE/1031 EXCHANGE

List the property for sale then use the proceeds to purchase a replacement property via a 1031 Exchange. Let's assume a sale price of $2.625MM and sale costs of 6.0%, with $1,207,500 in equity to use to purchase a replacement property, as calculated below:

Sale Price	$ 2,625,000
Less Sale Costs (6.0%)	$ (157,500)
Less Existing Loans	$ (1,260,000)
Proceeds for a 1031	**$ 1,207,500**

Based on the requirements of a 1031 Exchange, you need to replace all $1,260,000 in debt (remember, we had an Interest-Only loan, so no principal was paid down). Assuming you could purchase a replacement property with 30% down, your $1,207,500 would be enough to purchase a property worth $3,850,000 with some funds left for closing costs, as calculated below:

Down Payment = $3,850,000 * 30% = $1,155,000
Funds for closing costs = $1,207,500 - $1,155,000 = $52,500

Once you purchase your replacement property for $3,850,000 at a 6.0% CAP, your NOI and Pre-Tax Cash Flow will increase as well. Your new NOI will be $231,000 and your Pre-Tax Cash Flow will be $69,300, calculated as follows:

NOI = CAP Rate * Property Value = $3,850,000 * .06 = $231,000
Pre-Tax Cash Flow = NOI - Debt Service
Debt Service = New Loan * Interest Rate = ($3,850,000 - $1,155,000)
* .06 = $161,700
Pre-Tax Cash Flow = $231,000 - $161,700 = $69,300

You new property will look as follows:

Market Value	$ 3,850,000
Debt	$ 2,695,000
Equity	$ 1,155,000
Pre-Tax Cash Flow	$ 69,300

Your new cash-on-cash return, or ROI, will be 5.7%, calculated as follows:

ROI = Pre-Tax Cash Flow/(Down Payment + Closing Costs)
ROI = $69,300/($1,155,000 + $52,500) = 5.7%

Also, your ROE will be 5.7% since, at time of purchase, the ROI and ROE are equal.

By selling your property and doing a 1031 Exchange, you're able to replace a property you purchased for $1.8MM with a property valued at $3.85MM and increase your original equity from $540,000 to $1,155,000. Now, let's see how Option 2 looks.

OPTION 2 - CASH-OUT REFI

Instead of selling, you consult with your mortgage broker about doing a cash-out refi. The new loan is based on the current NOI, interest rate, and DCR used by the lender. We know that the NOI is $157,500 per year. Based on a 1.15 DCR and a 6.0% interest rate, you'd qualify for a $1,885,000 loan, calculated as follows:

NOI	$157,500
DCR	1.15
Interest Rate	6.00%
Maximum Debt Service	$136,957
Maximum Loan Amount	$1,885,183
Current Loan	$1,260,000
Cash Out	$625,183

Once you pay off the existing mortgage of $1,260,000, you're left with $625,000. Assuming it costs you $25,000 to originate the loan, you'd have $600,000 in equity to invest. If we follow the same exercise we used in Option 1 above, this $600,000 could buy you the following:

Total Equity to Invest	$	600,000
Purchase Price	$	1,900,000
Down Payment	$	570,000
Closing Costs	$	30,000
NOI	$	114,000
Debt Service	$	79,800
Pre-Tax Cash Flow	$	34,200
ROI		5.7%

After your refi, your portfolio would look like this:

		Building 1	Building 2	Total
Market Value	$	2,625,000 $	1,900,000 $	4,525,000
Debt	$	1,885,000 $	1,330,000 $	3,215,000
Equity	$	740,000 $	570,000 $	1,310,000
Pre-Tax Cash Flow	$	44,390 $	34,200 $	78,590

And, you now own *two* properties worth over $4MM generating a Pre-Tax Cash Flow of over $78,000.

The real question then is, "Which option is better?" Here are the results side by side:

Option 1 - Sale/1031

Market Value	$	3,850,000
Debt	$	2,695,000
Equity	$	1,155,000
Pre-Tax Cash Flow	$	69,300

Option 2 - Cash-out Refi/New Purchase

		Building 1	Building 2	Total
Market Value	$	2,625,000 $	1,900,000 $	4,525,000
Debt	$	1,885,000 $	1,330,000 $	3,215,000
Equity	$	740,000 $	570,000 $	1,310,000
Pre-Tax Cash Flow	$	44,390 $	34,200 $	78,590

Option 2 has the edge in all categories. Your portfolio has a larger market value, more equity, and a larger Pre-Tax Cash Flow. The only negative would be you have $500,000 more in debt. Given the above results, Option 2 makes more sense. It's also the easier option since you don't have to market your property for sale and then be constrained by the guidelines of a 1031 Exchange when looking for your replacement property. Also, you can initiate a cash-out refi at your convenience and use the proceeds to find a property when the right one comes along, not within the 45- or 180-day time frame required by a 1031 Exchange.

Remember, Options 1 and 2 are a result of starting out with a property you purchased for $1.8MM with $540,000 down. Both options more than double the value of your real estate portfolio, and help you take a step up the next rung of your Property Ladder.

Whenever you consider a sale or cash-out refi, you always want to consider all options and model all scenarios in Excel. It's far easier to make an educated decision once you have the figures in front of you. In this example, there doesn't seem to be any reason to sell and do a 1031 Exchange; however, that's not always the case. Sometimes you're ready to sell and move on. You might be tired of the tenant base (difficult to manage, bounce their rent checks, etc.); the neighborhood may be iffy (declining or dangerous); the property may be aging and requires more repairs; or the property may be further away than you'd like (too long a drive or out of state).

One final reason you'd want to sell and do a 1031 Exchange over doing a cash-out refi is that you've exhausted the depreciation on your property. In order to do this, you'd have to have owned a multi-family property for at least 27.5 years and/or a commercial property for 39 years. If you have, you no longer have any Depreciation Expense to deduct and shield your Pre-Tax Cash Flow with. All of these are valid, compelling reasons that owners sell rather than do a cash-out refi and hold a property. In fact, you only want to consider the cash-out refi scenario if you like the property you own and want to keep it. If you don't, then the Sale/1031 option is probably best.

As the example above illustrates, the Property Ladder is a very powerful concept. By taking the equity you've accrued through appreciation and NOI growth (rent growth), you can purchase more and larger properties, continually increasing your Pre-Tax Cash Flow and the overall value of your portfolio. In order to accomplish this, it's imperative you continually evaluate your portfolio and be prepared to either sell or refinance the properties you own. If you're too lazy or don't pay attention, you'll let valuable opportunities slip away.

CHAPTER 14 – CONDO CONVERSIONS & GROUND-UP CONSTRUCTION: AVOIDING THE POTHOLES

This book wouldn't be complete if I didn't spend some time discussing Condo Conversions and Ground-Up Construction projects. These two categories of real estate investments are considered some of the riskiest, and with good reason. In both cases you invest in a project that generates no monthly income during the hold period; and requires you to accurately project how the residential real estate market will be doing sometime in the future, usually months, if not years, after you close escrow on the purchase. Because of this, I suggest only experienced investors invest in these types of deals, and that you make sure you spend time and energy carefully scrutinizing the underlying assumptions being made by the Developer or General Partner.

CONDO CONVERSIONS

Condo Conversions are when you purchase an existing multi-family property and entitle it to *for-sale product*. Though I described this in Chapter 7, let's revisit my example of when I invested in a 25-unit condo conversion in LA County. When we purchased the property, it was operating as a 25-unit apartment building with 25 separate tenants and one APN (Assessor's Parcel Number). Our goal was to purchase the building then go to the City of Los Angeles and apply for a Tentative Tract Map. The names of the legal documents will vary by locale, but essentially, we were requesting that the City allow us to subdivide the property into 25 separate APNs, or parcels. By doing this, we'd then be able to sell off each unit to individual owners. The reason anyone would want to undertake this endeavor is because as a bulk purchase, we paid $6.0MM for the 25-units, but as individual units, they were worth as much as $10.2MM, or more.

In order to get the necessary City approvals to entitle the property as for-sale condominiums, there was a lengthy and expensive process that was required. Again, this process varies by locale; but in the City of Los Angeles, the process can take from 12-24 months and cost upwards of a few hundred thousand dollars. Once the City grants approval to convert the units to condos, you need to vacate all the tenants and rehab the interior and exterior of the property from apartment-quality to condo-quality since homeowners expect a higher level of finishes for a property they own rather than rent. Costs to do this can range from a few thousand dollars per unit, to upwards of $50,000 or more. Our project had 25 units, and we spent a total of $1.15MM between the entitlement process with the City and the property rehab. Funds were allocated as follows:

Entitlement Process with City/State	$ 225,000
Interior Rehab ($25,000/unit)	$ 625,000
Exterior Rehab	$ 300,000
Total Costs	**$1,150,000**

Additionally, we had financing costs since we did not pay all cash for the property, and had borrowed debt. The total project cost was estimated to be approximately $7.15MM at the outset. At the time we purchased the property, the lender was willing to finance 80% of the project cost with a loan, and the other 20% would come in the form of our down payment. The interest rate the bank was charging was 9.0%, and the term of the loan was 18 months. Our financing costs looked as follows:

Loan Amount = $7.15MM *.80 = $5,720,000
Interest Expense = $5,720,000 *.09% * 18 months = $772,200

Our total projects costs looked as follows:

Entitlement Process with City/State	$ 225,000
Interior Rehab ($25,000/unit)	$ 625,000
Exterior Rehab	$ 300,000
Total Costs	**$1,150,000**
Plus Financing Costs	$ 772,200
Plus Property Cost	$6,000,000
Total Project Costs	**$7,922,200**

Our Total Project Costs equaled $7,922,200; however, this did not include our costs of sale, which varied based on the sale price of each unit. As you know, whenever you sell a piece of real estate, you're going to have sale costs including, but not limited to, broker's fees, title/escrow, and city and county transfer taxes. In addition, we also spent money on marketing materials. On our project, these costs amounted to 6.8% of our total retail value, which ended up being $10.2MM. The total retail value of the project is simply the summation of the sale prices of all individual units; and, our Total Sale Costs equaled:

Total Sale Costs = 6.8% * $10.2MM = $694,000

So, our total profit was calculated as follows:

Total Retail Value	$10,200,000
Less Total Project Costs	$ 7,922,200
Less Total Sale Costs	$ 694,000
Gross Profit	**$ 1,583,800**

Remember, the total Capital invested was 20% of $7.15MM, or $1,430,000. In this project, as in most Condo Conversions and Ground-Up Construction deals, there was a General Partner and multiple Limited Partners. The General Partner sourced the deal, raised the Capital, procured the financing, obtained the entitlements for the project, and oversaw the rehab and sale of the units. In return for doing all of this, he invested $0 and retained 50% of the project. So, he earned $791,900 (50% of $1,583,300) in 18 months, and the other $791,900 was returned to investors. The investors earned a 55.8% ROI, calculated as follows:

ROI = Profit to Investors/Total Capital Invested by Investors = $791,900/$1,430,000 = 55.8%

The annualized return, since the project took 18 months, equaled 34%.

A 34% IRR is an *excellent* return for any project, and far exceeds the IRRs you typically earn on a multi-family or NNN property. However, there is much more risk associated with these types of projects. If the residential market were to *soften* and prices were to fall by even 5% over the 18-month entitlement/rehab period, the project would earn $510,000 less, and the investors' ROI would fall from 55.8% to 37.8%, calculated as follows:

Retail Sellout Discount = 5% * $10.2MM = $510,000
Gross Profit - Retail Sellout Discount = $1,583,800 - $510,000 = $1,073,800
Return to Investors = .5 * $1,073,800 = $536,900
Investors' ROI = $536,900/$1,430,000 = 37.5%

Recall that in the earlier example, the investors' ROI was 55.8%. As you can see, a small shift in the residential market can have a huge impact on a project's ROI.

One major benefit of Condo Conversions is that if the residential market does fall and you're unable to sell the rehabbed units, you still retain the option of renting them, thereby generating income to use to pay your mortgage. At this point, you'll probably be able to collect more monthly rent than you did before since the units have been rehabbed to condo-quality. Also, you'd want to talk to the bank about replacing your A&D loan with a permanent loan at a lower interest rate because, typically, A&D loans carry a 2%-3% higher interest rate than a permanent loan.

GROUND-UP CONSTRUCTION

Ground-Up Construction projects face the same challenges as Condo Conversions, and more. With these projects you're usually purchasing vacant land that may or may not be entitled to build what you'd like. If the project is not entitled, you need to hire an architect and engineer then go the City with plans to start and go through the approval process. The time required varies by locale, but expect a minimum of 12 months and as many as a few years or more in less development-friendly areas. In Santa Monica, CA, the entitlement and approval process can easily *average* 3-4 years; and throughout this time, your property is sitting vacant, which means it's not generating any income for you.

These types of projects not only usually take longer than Conversions, but can be more Capital-intensive. Since the time between the initial purchase of the land and the completion of the structure can stretch for years, you take a far greater sellout risk with regards to timing the market. Unlike a Conversion project that has value as a rental, if a developer goes bankrupt on a Ground-Up project before it's complete, he has no way to generate any monthly rental income to pay his mortgage with while he waits for the market to come back.

There are many factors in these types of projects and investments that are not easily controlled by the developer. The retail market may soften, construction costs may increase, material costs can rise, and absorption rates can slow. Let's look at each of these.

The retail market can soften. In late 2006, the residential market started showing the first signs of a slow down and has continued on through 2008, with prices falling by 15%-20% or more in many areas.

Construction costs can increase. In Southern California, beginning in early 2003, construction costs rose at a rapid pace due to all the new development going on in the local area, Las Vegas, and the world. In fact, with all the condominium towers being built in Las Vegas, all of the construction crews within a 500-mile radius were being employed, driving up the cost of labor for everyone.

Material costs can increase. Since early 2003, the cost of concrete, steel, and copper have more than *doubled* due to the huge global demand for these goods, mainly driven by China's 6%+ annual growth rate.

Absorption rates can slow. Absorption rates are how long it takes for the market to absorb new product. In this example, how long does it take to sell 25 new condos? When the project was first purchased and the real estate market was more vibrant, the developer had projected a 6-month absorption rate, or selling 4 units each month. By the time the project was ready to be sold, however, the real estate market had slowed considerably and so had absorption rates, with the project taking 9 months instead of 6. Those extra 3 months of time did not come cheaply since the meter was still ticking on the loan, which was being repaid at a 9% interest rate.

As you can see, any one of these factors can greatly influence the outcome of a project; but when you combine two or more, the project can go from being a *home run* to a loser very quickly. And typically, these factors don't occur by themselves, but in groups.

While I don't recommend these types of riskier investments for everyone, they can be part of a balanced real estate portfolio. I have about 10%-15% of my assets in these types of deals, with those funds invested over multiple projects. I suggest that younger investors steer clear of these opportunities; and for every investor, *never* invest funds you can't afford to lose. There's always a chance they won't be returned due to market conditions.

Also, you want to make sure that the ownership structure is such that your liability is limited to your total investment, and no more. If a project were to go bust, it's very possible the developer would need to file bankruptcy and may owe many contractors lots of money. In that case, you don't want to be financially liable for any of the debts. You just want to be able to walk away and regroup, having lost your investment, but that's all.

CHAPTER 15 — WORKING WITH REAL ESTATE BROKERS AND MORTGAGE LENDERS: KEYS TO A SUCCESSFUL RELATIONSHIP

Now that you've got the tools to analyze and underwrite a deal, you're ready to start working with real estate brokers and lenders. Brokers are your lifeline to what's going on in your prospective marketplace(s) or investment area(s). They provide you with current listings, information on recently sold properties, and market trends you can use to project future growth and opportunities. It's important that you establish relationships with your local brokerage and lending community as you'll be relying on these professionals to help you identify potential opportunities and get them financed.

There are several national commercial brokerages that have a strong presence in most markets. These include Re/Max Commercial, Marcus & Millichap, CBRE, Sperry Van Ness, and Colliers Seeley. This is by no means a comprehensive list, and there are many other well qualified brokerage firms you can research. The firms I listed, however, have a large national presence with offices throughout the United States, and in some cases the world. My suggestion is for you to do a search of the brokerage firms in your area and identify the top three or four. One of the best ways to do this is to visit a website called Loopnet at www.loopnet.com. Loopnet is an invaluable resource and is the equivalent of a national MLS for commercial properties. Listings are posted and updated daily by commercial brokers looking to expose their listings to as broad an audience as possible. Anyone, anywhere can access Loopnet, free of charge. You can search by property type (i.e., Multi-Family, Retail, Office, etc.), as well as geographical location and price. Loopnet is a great resource to begin your search; and, it will help you identify the most active brokers in your area by allowing you to see how many listings they currently have for sale.

As an active commercial broker myself, I can tell you that part of my daily job is the cultivation of new business, which basically amounts to warm- and cold-calling to find new clients. I'm always looking to meet seasoned and new investors interested in purchasing investment property whom I can lend my expertise to. As a new investor yourself, I suggest you prepare a short resume that details any real estate-related experience you have, as well as the amount of capital you currently have to work with and what type of investment you're interested in. Then, you should contact three to four of the most active agents in your area by phone and/or email and introduce yourself. You can do this by emailing them a quick note with your resume, followed by a voicemail requesting a call back. Once you've spoken, you might even suggest a time to get together or grab lunch. Establishing a personal connection can go a long way to ensure you're top-of-mind with your broker when great deals become available. Remember, though, that the top brokers are usually quite busy; so getting in front of them, especially if you're a novice investor with limited resources, may prove challenging.

I've always been big on responsiveness and customer service, so advise you to lean towards working with brokers who return your calls and emails in a prompt fashion. Remember, you want to meet as many active brokers as possible so when new deals come on the market, they call or email you right away to alert you about them. Speed can be an advantage in this business; and often brokers will share *pocket listings* with you before they're exposed to the broader market.

Pocket Listings are usually deals that brokers know are for sale but they do not have Exclusive Listing Agreements for. The broker has spoken with a Seller who has an interest in selling at the right price, but isn't ready to list his property. This can present an opportunity for the right investor since the property will probably be sold without exposure to the entire market. Because of this, there may be less competition for the property, which can result in a lower price and better deal for the investor. I've sold many deals this way in my career and it remains a consistent part of my business.

Your intent when you first speak with any agent is to tell him about yourself, your investment experience and goals, your source and amount of available capital, and your time frame to invest. Brokers have limited time to work with hundreds of clients, so they prioritize investors based on available funds and time period to invest. If client A is looking to buy immediately (and in a 1031 Exchange with only 45 days to identify a replacement property) while client B is looking to purchase in the next 3-6 months, most brokers spend more time and energy helping client A since a paycheck is far more likely and comes sooner than later. This is the reality of any sales-driven business; so rather than getting frustrated about it, take advantage of it. If your time frame is not immediate, stay in touch with the broker on a weekly basis. Let him know you're still looking and include your investment criteria each time as a reminder to him. Follow up with a phone call once a month to keep in touch.

As a broker, I can tell you that I always appreciate investors who stay in touch with me. It makes my job easier, lets me know how motivated they are, and reminds me that they're still searching for their next investment. After all, the job of a broker can be overwhelming at times; and keeping track of hundreds of potential investors that you don't connect with regularly can be daunting, if not unrealistic.

Once you've established a relationship with some *real estate brokers* you feel comfortable working with, you want to get recommendations for some local *mortgage brokers* so you establish those relationships as well. There are three great sources for these referrals: Real estate brokers you work with, fellow investors, and local banks. When working with any new client, one of the first items I always discuss is financing and who, if anyone, they work with. Financing is one of the most important parts of any investment since most investors do not pay all cash for a property. Therefore, it's important you have a couple of go-to lenders who are familiar with your financial background and you're comfortable doing business with. Just as with your real estate agent, you want to speak with potential lenders a few times and provide them with your financial information and investment goals. They can help you navigate the financial markets and discuss available lending options based on the property type you're considering.

When you receive a potential investment opportunity from your agent to review, you want to forward it onto your lender so he can underwrite the deal and let you know which financing options are available to you—which is why you want to already have a relationship(s) established.

As you can see, part of being a successful real estate investor is to create a network of professionals you rely on for information and expertise. Your real estate brokers will provide you with available listings, local market knowledge, and market trends. Your lenders will keep you abreast of new financial products available, as well as current lending rates and underwriting guidelines. It's important to stay current since *little* things like DCR ratios can change substantially and completely alter your ability to finance a property. For example, in April 2007, many local Los Angeles banks were underwriting refinances to a 1.0 DCR, essentially a break-even ratio. By September

2007, just 5 months later, and after the summer 2007 sub-prime meltdown, all banks had to significantly tighten their underwriting guidelines and went back to a more normal DCR ratio of 1.15. That small change greatly affected the loan proceeds on any deal (making them smaller) and slowed the pace of deal flow in the market since financing had become harder to obtain.

LOOPNET, THE MLS, AND OTHER ONLINE WEBSITES

The Internet has greatly changed how most industries do business; and real estate is no exception. There are many great online resources available for you to take advantage of. Below is a list of some of the sites I use frequently. This list is by no means comprehensive, and there are probably hundreds more I haven't even heard of. In fact, you'd be amazed at how much information you can find from a simple Google search. My suggestion is to visit the sites below first; and if you can't find what you are looking for, search elsewhere. You want to establish a go-to list of online resources you rely on for quick information, as needed.

MLS (Multiple Listing Service) - The MLS is a local depot for residential and small (2- to 4-unit) multi-family listings. This is typically the best place for you to find information on SFRs and 2- to 4-unit properties for sale in your area. MLSs are usually organized locally, either by city or county; and more often than not, access is password-protected. If you're in the market for a 2- to 4-unit property, you want to contact a local residential agent you feel comfortable working with to gain access to these sites. MLSs are not national in nature, and you usually need to do a Google search to find the url of the local MLS you're searching for.

Loopnet.com - Loopnet is the commercial equivalent of the MLS, except that it is national in nature. Unlike the MLS, you don't need a password to search on Loopnet, so anyone can gain access to properties all across the country. It's a great place to search for any type of income property from multi-family to retail, to commercial to office. You can search by price, geography, and product type. You can also search for leases. There are numerous other sites that "compete" with Loopnet. In my experience, they cull the majority of their listings from Loopnet and simply repackage the information in a less user-friendly manner. Loopnet is by far the best online resource I've found and is the site most widely-used by real estate brokers and professionals across the United States.

In addition to the above property listing sites, there are numerous other sites that provide access to local market data and trends, as well as tax loopholes and all things real estate-related. Some of the sites I've visited and found useful include:

www.dataquick.com – Great for local data, home sales, median pricing, etc.

www.taxloopholes.com – Just as it sounds, a resource for better understanding the IRS tax code and how you can keep more money in your pocket.

www.wsj.com (*Wall Street Journal*) – This is a great national paper that keeps you up-to-date on national and global events. While real estate is a local investment, national and global events affect pricing and financing; so, it's best to keep abreast with what's happening around the US and world.

SFR Info/Value

http://realtor.com
http://www.housevalues.com
http://www.zillow.com

Demographic Info

http://www.census.gov/geo/www/fips/fips65
http://www.census.gov
http://www.vandema.com/Stats.htm
http://adage.com/americandemographics

Mortgage Calculator

http://www.bankrate.com/brm/mortgage-calculator.asp

Real Estate Tools

http://realestate.aol.com
http://realestate.yahoo.com
http://realestate.msn.com
http://www.moving.com
http://realestate.iwon.com/index.html

http://msnbc.homepages.com/Home.aspx
http://www.usatoday.com/marketplace/realestate/front.htm
www.zilpy.com
www.dothomes.com

Housing Research and Information

http://www.dqnews.com
http://www.huduser.org
http://www.ofheo.gov/HPI.asp
http://www.realestateeconomics.com
http://www.realestatejournal.com
http://money.cnn.com/real_estate/index.html

Economy

http://cbsnews.com/htdocs/economy/framesource.html
http://money.cnn.com/news/economy/index.html
http://www.forbes.com/economy
http://www.bls.gov/eag/eag.us.htm
http://www.whitehouse.gov/infocus/economy
http://www.economy.com/dismal
http://www.wn.com/economy

Loans

http://www.mortgagecalc.com
http://www.federalreserve.gov

In Los Angeles, we have two great publications that I subscribe to. The first is the *California Real Estate Journal* and the other is the *Los Angeles Business Journal*. The first provides me with great information on purely real estate-related topics throughout the state, and the second provides me with great business information on Los Angeles County which is where I conduct 90% of my business and investing. Both help keep me up-to-date on the local market and trends. I suggest you find out which local journals are in your area, and subscribe to them.

One of the best ways to stay ahead of the game in real estate, or any industry, is to be well read and informed. There's a wealth of information available on the Internet, and a majority of it can be obtained for free. Spend some time finding out which local resources are available in your area and bookmark those pages. Sign up for email alerts and newsletters. Attend local forums and interact with fellow investors. Consider starting your own investment club that meets weekly or monthly. Do what you can to stay as close to the business as possible so that when you're financially ready to purchase your next (or first) investment, you're prepared and have all the information and contacts you need.

CHAPTER 16 – A FINAL NOTE: YOUR FIRST STEP IN A LIFELONG JOURNEY

Now that you've completed this book, your real journey is about to begin. If you're like most investors, you've started looking for your first deal and are eager to make a purchase. Remember, it's better to pass on a good deal than jump at a bad one. I can't tell you how many of my students at UCLA come into my class chomping at the bit to buy something—anything—and I always advise them to exercise patience. It's taken them a long time to save up the capital they have to invest and they could blow it on their first deal if they're not careful. Most of them only have $20,000-50,000 ready to invest, which in our LA market, is usually not enough. So, I preach *patience* and *education*.

My suggestion is to reread this book, or specific chapters, as needed. Use it as a reference guide in your investing career. Some chapters will have little relevance to you right now, such as the chapter on 1031 Exchanges, but will become more important once you're ready and at that stage of your investing career. And, never stop learning. Talk to other investors like yourself, find a local investment club, or start one. Initiate conversations with local real estate agents and mortgage brokers, and go online and research the area(s) where you're interested in investing. Stay close to the real estate market so that when the right opportunity comes along, you're ready to take advantage of it.

If you haven't already done so, consider purchasing the 13 Chapter DVD series I've created which walks you through most of the chapters in this book. Each video is 15-35 minutes long and will help to reinforce the concepts discussed in this book. This is a great way for you to master some of the more difficult concepts, especially those contained in Chapters 8, 9 and 10. You can purchase the videos by visiting www.theresnofreelunchinrealestate.com. And, if you're ready to take your investing career to the next level, contact me to learn more about one-on-one coaching. This is a great way for you to have me walk you through your first deal, or help you analyze possible purchase, cash-out refi or 1031 Exchange scenarios.

There's a saying I'm very fond of: "Luck favors the prepared." We all know investors who've made millions in real estate, and it's easy to attribute their success to luck. But, I guarantee you that if you were to learn more about their journey, you'd come to find out they spent *many hours* researching investments before they made a buying decision.

My journey in real estate began in late 2001, and it's been a wild ride. I've had a lot of fun, met some great people, and have been fortunate to amass some wealth. Like you, my quest for knowledge never ends and every person I meet presents an opportunity for me to learn from their experiences. I like to tell my students that if I were to win the Lottery tomorrow, I'd still do what I do—because I love it. Real estate is my passion and the art of the deal energizes me. Creating wealth and an ever-growing passive income stream exhilarates me and I want to continue to share that passion with others.

I hope you've enjoyed this book and benefited by learning more about real estate investing than you knew before. Let this be the first step in your journey to creating the life you want and the wealth you desire.